10/07

A **FALCON** GUIDE®

D0149919

Best Easy Day Hikes Series

Best Easy Day Hikes Zion and Bryce Canyon National Parks

Erik Molvar and Tamara Martin

FALCON GUIDES®

GUILFORD, CONNECTICUT
HELENA, MONTANA

AN IMPRINT OF THE GLOBE PEQUOT PRESS

To buy books in quantity for corporate use
or incentives, call **(800) 962–0973**
or e-mail **premiums@GlobePequot.com**.

For Mad Melanie, the Night Hiker of Zion,
and for Jamie for his love.

Contents

Acknowledgments

First of all, we would like to thank the residents of Long Valley for their outstanding hospitality during the course of our research. Myrna Cox and her family, of Glendale, were particularly helpful in our search for a place to live. Thanks also to Cleve and Lorene Esplin and to the Chamberlains for sharing their fascinating stories with us. Steven Robinson was a wellspring of information about Cedar Breaks National Monument. Thanks also to Rod Schipper of the Bureau of Land Management's Kanab office for his geological insights. Dan Habig of Zion National Park provided interpretive information for this book, and Jerry Davis oversaw the review process for that part of the book. Thanks to Paula Henrie of Bryce Canyon National Park for reviewing the Bryce Canyon section. We would also like to thank our respective families, particularly Kathy, James, John, and Ginger, for their never-ending patience, support, and love throughout all of our adventures.

Help Us Keep This Guide Up to Date

Every effort has been made by the authors and editors to make this guide as accurate and useful as possible. However, many things can change after a guide is published—trails are rerouted, regulations change, facilities come under new management, etc.

We would love to hear from you concerning your experiences with this guide and how you feel it could be improved and kept up to date. While we may not be able to respond to all comments and suggestions, we'll take them to heart and we'll also make certain to share them with the authors. Please send your comments and suggestions to the following address:

> The Globe Pequot Press
> Reader Response/Editorial Department
> P.O. Box 480
> Guilford, CT 06437

Or you may e-mail us at:

> editorial@GlobePequot.com

Thanks for your input, and happy trails!

Introduction

The southwestern corner of Utah offers some of the most fascinating and awe-inspiring landscapes in the desert Southwest. Towering cliffs and slickrock canyons, with colorful spires and natural arches, exist here on a scale that dwarfs the works of humans and provides a humbling time scale by which to measure our own histories. Half a billion years in the making, this land was laid down in seas and lakes and dunes, then thrust skyward to be sculpted by the ceaseless efforts of wind and water. Here the visitor finds refuge from the fast-paced modern world, in a country little changed for a thousand years.

Weather

Southwestern Utah encompasses low deserts, arid uplands, and high, subalpine forestlands. There is no time of year when good hiking opportunities cannot be had.

Winters are cool and rainy at the lower elevations, but the high plateaus are typically locked in deep snowdrifts from November through April. Despite the snow, Bryce Canyon National Park is open year-round. Some of its day-hiking trails may remain passable throughout the winter, but deep snows collect in other areas.

Cedar Breaks and the rest of the Markagunt Plateau are completely snowbound and inaccessible to hikers during the winter. The uplands of Zion National Park typically are closed to entry during winter, although the Zion Canyon area remains open. Water temperatures are usually too low during winter to allow wading for extended periods.

The hallmark of spring is melting snow. Streams in this otherwise desert region become swollen with runoff, making many of the canyon hikes impassable. The high country is still snowbound at this time, although the Kolob Terrace of Zion National Park begins to open up in late April. The low deserts receive much of their annual rainfall in the spring, when they burst into a colorful display of blossoms. However, the moist soils of the low desert are prone to sticky mud at this time, which makes cross-country hiking an unpleasant activity—as well as one that can damage the environment. Spring is an excellent time to visit Bryce Canyon: Its cliffs and hoodoos are even prettier with a light dusting of snow.

Sweltering summer temperatures make hiking at midday toilsome, especially in the lower elevations. Confine your hiking to early morning and evening hours to avoid the worst of the heat. Savvy hikers retreat into the shady depths of the canyons or up to the breezy subalpine country atop the plateaus to beat the heat. The region experiences dry weather through the first half of summer, but late August is known for torrential thunderstorms that can trigger flash floods in the slot canyons and create spectacular waterfalls on the cliffs. Lightning strikes along the rims of the Bryce Canyon and Cedar Breaks amphitheaters are also a serious hazard at this time.

Autumn is perhaps the best time of year to visit the region. Temperatures are warm during the day, with frigid, crystal-clear nights. Water levels in the canyons are low at this time, and the water temperature remains fairly constant until late October, when it begins to plummet. As a bonus, travelers along the waterways are treated to colorful displays from the turning maples and cottonwoods, and visitors to the high country can take in the brilliant gold foliage of the aspens. The highest plateaus enjoy cool autumn weather but generally remain snow-free until mid-October. The lower terraces and canyon bottoms are warm and temperate at this time. Temperatures in the low desert of southwestern Zion become tolerable in late October.

Hiking in Arid Lands

Hiking in the Southwest poses challenges that are encountered nowhere else. Much of southwestern Utah's public land is free of trails, and hikers may have to rely on their map and compass skills to find their way. The defining feature of the region is "slickrock," in which vast expanses of sculpted sandstone have been scoured bare by wind and water. As its name suggests, slickrock can be very slippery when it gets wet. Trails and routes that cross slickrock will be marked only with cairns, if they are marked at all. Hikers who travel through canyons should remain constantly aware that it is much easier to climb up a slickrock face than it is to descend one.

Perhaps the most obvious challenge in desert hiking is the extreme weather. During the hottest parts of the day, the temperature can reach 120 degrees Fahrenheit several feet above the floor of the low desert. Summer hikers should wear broad-brimmed hats, long-sleeved shirts, and baggy pants to protect themselves from the intensity of the desert sun. Cover exposed skin with sunscreen lotion. Take a lesson from the local wildlife—hike in the cool of the mornings and evenings, and rest in the shade during the heat of the day.

The desert air wicks moisture away from the body at an amazing rate, and active hikers should plan to drink about a gallon of water per day. Desert water sources may run dry for part of the year and often contain exotic microbes that can cause intestinal disorders. Always carry enough water to meet your daily needs, and filter all surface water before drinking to remove the harmful microbes.

Many desert-dwelling animals have evolved poisons, and they may bite or sting when provoked. The rattlesnake is the most notorious of these, although its reputation for aggressiveness is undeserved. This nocturnal predator will flee when given a chance, and it rarely bites unless it is surprised or cornered. To avoid snakebites, always watch where you put your hands and feet, and avoid reaching into dark places or overturning boulders. This practice will also help you avoid scorpions, most of which have painful stings. Scorpions like to hide in dark, moist places; hikers who leave their boots outside overnight may be in for a nasty surprise in the morning.

Desert hikers must be particularly careful not to upset the ecological balance of desert communities. Many plants and animals live on the edge of their capabilities, and any added stress may result in death. Give a wide berth to nesting birds, animals with young, and wildlife that is using a water source. Finally, hikers who are traveling in the low desert or piñon-juniper scrubland should avoid walking on biological soil crusts. These crusts are dark and granular and contain algae and other microbes that come alive following rains. A major source of nutrients for desert soils, they form a crucial link in the web of desert ecosystems. Biological soil crusts are very fragile and may not recover for decades after being trampled.

Sharing the Trail

Visitors should expect to encounter a wide variety of user groups in southwestern Utah, particularly on Bureau of

Land Management and National Forest lands. This magnificent wilderness is a magnet for outdoor folk and solitude seekers of all descriptions. In the interest of a safe and pleasant wilderness experience for all, exercise consideration and good manners when meeting other parties on the trail.

Pack and saddle stock have the right-of-way on the trails wherever they are allowed. Because pack and saddle stock are less maneuverable than foot travelers, hikers should yield to horse parties when the two meet on a trail. In such a situation, the best thing that a hiker can do is to hike up the hillside above the trail for at least 20 feet and allow the stock to pass. It often helps to talk to the animals in reassuring tones as they pass by. This keeps the animals from panicking and tangling up the pack string.

How to Follow a Faint Path

Many of the most popular treks in this corner of Utah exist only as primitive routes that may not be marked at all. Visitors to backcountry areas should have a few elementary trail-finding skills in their bag of tricks, in case a trail peters out or a snowfall covers the path. A topographic map and compass, and the ability to use them, are essential insurance against disaster when a trail takes a wrong turn or disappears completely.

Maintained trails in southwestern Utah are typically marked in a variety of ways. Signs bearing the name and/or number of the trail are present at some trail junctions, although weathering and inconsiderate visitors sometimes remove these plaques. Along the trail several kinds of markers indicate the location of maintained trails. In forested areas, cuts in the bark of living trees, known as blazes, are made immediately beside the path. In spots where a trail crosses a gravel streambed or bare slickrock, piles of rocks called cairns mark the route. These cairns are typically constructed of three or more stones piled atop one another, a formation that almost never occurs naturally.

In the case of an extremely overgrown trail, markings of any kind may be impossible to find. On such a trail the techniques used to build the trail serve as clues to its location. Well-constructed trails have rather wide, flat beds. Let your feet seek the flat spots when traveling through tall brush, and you will almost always find yourself on the trail. Look for check dams and other rock work on the trail that may have been put in place to prevent erosion. Old sawed logs from previous trail maintenance can be used to navigate in spots where the trail bed is obscured; if you find a sawed log, then you must be on a trail that was maintained at some point in time. Switchbacks are also a sure sign of an official trail; wild game travels in straight lines, and horsemen traveling off-trail seldom bother to zigzag across hillsides. Previous travelers can also leaves clues to the location of old trails; watch for footprints or hoof marks as you travel.

When attempting to find a trail that has disappeared, ask yourself where the most logical place would be to build a trail given its source and destination. Trail builders tend to seek level ground where it is available, and they often follow the natural contours of stream courses and ridgelines. Bear in mind that most trails avoid up-and-down motion in favor of long, sustained grades culminating in major passes or hilltops. Old trail beds can sometimes be spotted from a distance as they cut across hillsides at a constant angle.

Flash Floods and the Narrow Canyon Danger Level

In an area where soils are thin and bare rock covers much of the landscape, flash floods are an ever-present danger. Southwestern Utah is deeply scored with a network of spectacular channels that bear mute testimony to the erosive power of the floodwaters. Floodwaters grow in magnitude rather than dispersing when they enter slot canyons, and any living thing that stands in the way of the water is sure to be swept away. Although no foolproof method can guarantee your safety in a narrow canyon, hikers can take three basic steps to reduce the chances of being caught in a flash flood.

First, assess the danger before you begin your trip. If rain threatens or a moisture-laden weather system is expected to pass through, do not venture into canyon country. Zion National Park has developed the "Narrow Canyon Danger Level" as a measuring stick to predict the chances of a flash flood within the various parts of the park. This is specific to individual drainages within the park but may also be used as a general barometer for flash flood danger throughout the region. The Narrow Canyon Danger Level is updated each day and takes into account the latest weather reports and prevailing water levels. The danger levels can be interpreted as follows:

- **Low**—Favorable weather is in the forecast, but unexpected cloudbursts may nevertheless occur. This is the best time to hike a narrow canyon.
- **Moderate**—Flash flooding is a possibility, though not a strong one. High water levels may force some waist-deep wading and/or swimming.

- **High**—Canyon travel is not recommended. This rating is used when the danger of flooding is high, when existing water levels are up, or when the water is so cold that hypothermia is likely. If you choose to hike a canyon when a high danger level prevails, be sure to find out the exact nature of the danger and have a contingency plan that accounts for the worst-case scenario.

- **Extreme**—Canyon travel is closed due to hazardous conditions.

The second step is to continually reevaluate the potential for floods as you hike. Remember that a flood can occur under a clear blue sky if a downpour is in progress many miles away. Watch the skies for changing weather, and climb to safety or abort your hike if the clouds roll in. As you walk, watch the canyon walls for a muddy film and stranded driftwood that mark the high-water line during previous floods. Constantly scan the terrain for escape routes by which you can climb to safety above this high-water level. Also, keep your ears open. Flash floods make a muted roaring sound as they roll down a canyon, giving a few minutes' warning of the impending wall of water. An unaccountable roaring from upstream, often accompanied by a brisk and sudden wind, indicates the approach of floodwaters. Climb immediately to high ground.

The third step is to know how to escape floodwaters if they overtake you. The best course of action is to climb out of harm's way, but the sheer walls found in many slot canyons often make it impossible to climb above the water. If you cannot escape by climbing, seek out a side cleft where you can hide from the full fury of the floodwaters. Large boulders can also be used as shelter from floods—wedge your body behind the lee side of the rock so that you will not be swept away by the initial surge. Remember that floating debris is as dangerous as the water itself; if you are knocked unconscious, you will certainly drown.

Be prepared to rescue yourself and your companions in an emergency. Carry a supply of extra food when hiking in backcountry canyons in case you are trapped for several days by floodwaters.

Planning Your Trip

Reading this guidebook to the Zion and Bryce region is a good start, but wise hikers will gather as much current information as possible before starting out on a wilderness expedition. Permits are not required for expeditions into most of Utah's public lands, although they are required for backpacking and some day hikes in the national parks. It is always wise to check in with a local ranger station to get the latest report on trail conditions. Ask for the trail supervisor or recreation planner, who will be well prepared to answer your questions. A list of addresses and phone numbers for these ranger stations is provided in Appendix A at the back of this book.

The key to a quality hiking experience is good planning. Hikers who underestimate the distance or time required to complete a trip may find themselves hiking in the dark, a dangerous proposition at best. Each hike is accompanied by an estimated hiking time, calculated using an average speed of 2 miles per hour. And note that these rates do not include stops for rest and refreshment, which add tremendously to a hiker's enjoyment and appreciation of the surroundings.

Eight miles a day is a good goal for travelers new to backpacking, while old hands can generally cover 10 miles comfortably. We recommend traveling below top speed, focusing more attention on the surrounding natural beauty and less on the exercise of hiking itself. In addition, desert heat and aridity make it unwise to push one's limits.

Using This Guide

The primary intent of this FalconGuide is to provide information that will help hikers choose trips according to their desires and abilities, as well as a detailed description of each trail, interpreting its natural and historical features. This guide is intended to be used in conjunction with topographic maps, which can be purchased at ranger stations and at local gift and sporting goods stores, or through the U.S. Geological Survey, P.O. Box 25286, Federal Center, Denver, CO 80225. The USGS has stopped making the larger 15-minute map series and now publishes only 7.5-minute maps. Additionally, several fine topographic maps of larger areas have been published by various private organizations and are available in local stores.

In this book each trail description begins with an outline describing the physical characteristics of the trail. A general description of the trek comes first, followed by distance and the approximate hiking time. This description is followed by information on the best season for attempting the trail, which may be influenced by summer heat, winter snows, and/or wet season flooding.

Next is a difficulty rating. The rating can be interpreted as follows: Easy trails can be completed without difficulty by hikers of all abilities; hikes rated moderate will challenge novices; moderately strenuous hikes will tax even experienced hikers; and strenuous trails will push the physical limits of the most Herculean hiker.

Water availability along the trail is described next, according to its reliability. Even perennial, or year-round, water sources may dry up during drought years, and intermittent sources hold water only during the wet months. Wise hikers bring their own water rather than relying on natural supplies

Next, for some hikes, are comments on trail hazards and recommended equipment to bring along. These are followed by the appropriate 7.5-minute quadrangle topo maps for each featured hike, which are listed in plain type. Maps published by sources other than the USGS appear in italics. The managing agency responsible for the area is then listed under jurisdiction, and a brief set of directions for finding the trailhead rounds out the statistical section.

A detailed interpretive description of the trail—including geologic and ecological features, historical sites, campsites, and other important information—follows.

The Miles and Directions at the end of some hikes provide a mile-by-mile description of landmarks, trail junctions, and gradient changes. The official distances of the land management agency are presented for all trails that had them at press time. Where official distances were unavailable, they were developed using an instrument called a planimeter, which measures two-dimensional distances on a topographic map. These distances were then corrected for altitude gain or loss. The resulting mileages should be looked upon as conservative estimates because they may not account for small-scale twists and turns or minor ups and downs.

List of Hikes

From easiest to more challenging:

Temple of Sinawava, Hike 7
Rim Trail, Hike 13
West Bank of the Virgin River, Hike 4
Canyon Overlook, Hike 2
Bristlecone Loop, Hike 17
Red Hollow, Hike 20
Alpine Pond, Hike 12
Mossy Cave, Hike 18
Middle Fork of Taylor Creek, Hike 10
Navajo Loop, Hike 15
East Mesa, Hike 1
Emerald Pools, Hike 5
Northgate Peaks, Hike 9
Ramparts Trail—Spectra Point, Hike 11
Peekaboo Loop, Hike 16
The Watchman, Hike 3
Queens Garden—Sunrise to Sunset Points, Hike 14
Sugar Knoll–Red Cave, Hike 21
Red Canyon Loop, Hike 19
Coral Pink Sand Dunes, Hike 22
Eagle Crags, Hike 8
Angels Landing, Hike 6

Map Legend

Interstate	=84=	Trailhead	🔵1
U.S. Highway	=26=	Ranger Station	◣
State or County Road	=47=	Picnic Area	⊞
Gravel Road	═══	Campground	▲
Unimproved Road	=====	Cabins/Buildings	■
Peak/Elevation			▲ Bridge Mtn. *6,814 ft.*
Tunnel	▬▬	Falls	〜⸗
Featured Trail	▬▬▬▬	Corral	↻
Other Trail	---------	Cliffs	⬯⬯⬯⬯
Other X-C Route	··············	Overlook/Point of Interest	◨
River/Creek	〜〜	No-Camping Zone	▨
Intermittent Stream	-·-·-·		
Lake	⬭		
Spring	⚬		
Forest/Wilderness Boundary	▭		
Power Line	•—•—•		
Ruins	◰		

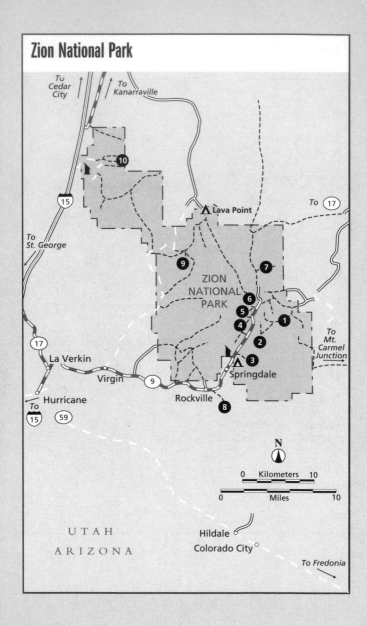

Zion National Park

To Cedar City
To Kanarraville

15

To St. George

17

La Verkin

Virgin

9

Rockville

Hurricane

To 15 59

10

Lava Point

9

ZION NATIONAL PARK

7

6
5
4
2
1

3
Springdale

8

To 17

To Mt. Carmel Junction

N

Kilometers
0 — 10

Miles
0 — 10

Hildale
Colorado City

UTAH
ARIZONA

To Fredonia

Zion National Park and Surrounding Lands

Z ion National Park encompasses the landscape of high plateaus, deep canyons, and sheer monoliths surrounding the North Fork of the Virgin River. It is a relatively small park that receives heavy visitation, particularly the day-hiking trails within Zion Canyon. Although the trails in this guide are single-day hikes, some are point-to-point hikes requiring more than one car.

Access to Zion Canyon is via Utah Highway 9, about 22 miles east of Hurricane and 25 miles west of Mount Carmel Junction. The main park campground and visitor center are at the mouth of the canyon. A scenic spur road ascends the canyon to access trailheads and the Zion Park Lodge. Since this area receives heavy use, the National Park Service has closed the road to private vehicles and now provides access by free shuttles. Currently, private shuttles transport hikers to the upper trailhead for The Narrows.

Hikers can reach the plateaus east of the canyon by trail from the Zion Ponderosa Ranch Resort, on the gravel road to Navajo Lake. The western part of the Kolob Terrace is accessible via the paved Kolob Reservoir Road, which departs from the highway at the town of Virgin. A primitive campground and a fire lookout manned by rangers can be found atop Lava Point. At the western edge of the Kolob Terrace are the Kolob Canyons, surrounded by spectacular towers of stone. Access them by a paved road from Interstate 15; a small visitor center here is permanently staffed by rangers.

The Zion Canyon Tram

The Park Service has instituted a shuttle service equipped with natural gas–powered trams to serve the popular Zion Canyon trailheads. The primary starting point for the tram is the main visitor center just east of Springdale, but during busy periods (when the visitor center parking lot is likely to be full), you can catch the tram at various marked points in the town of Springdale itself. There is no charge for the shuttle service, but riders are still required to pay the park entrance fee. The tram stops at Zion Canyon trailheads and points of interest four or more times each hour, from early morning to late evening. This shuttle service is fast and convenient, with plenty of room for backpacks.

1 East Mesa

A day hike offering access to Observation Point.

Distance: 8.0 miles (12.8 km) round-trip

Approximate hiking time: 4 hours

Best season: April through May; September through November

Difficulty: Easy

Water availability: None

Topo map: Temple of Sinawava; *Zion National Park* (ZNHA)

Jurisdiction: Zion National Park (See Appendix A for more information.)

Finding the trailhead: From Zion National Park's East Entrance, drive east on Utah Highway 9 for 2.4 miles to a junction with a paved road that runs north toward Navajo Lake and The Narrows trailhead. Turn left onto this road. After 5.3 miles the road arrives at the Zion Ponderosa Ranch Resort. Pass through the main entrance and drive west on the main route, which is Twin Knolls Road. The road ends at a T intersection; turn right and follow Beaver Road northward. This road deteriorates into a primitive track, which ultimately swings west to enter Zion National Park at the beginning of the East Mesa Trail.

The Hike

This trail to Observation Point is open to horses. The path begins by running west from the national park boundary through an open stand of ponderosa pine. Lightning strikes are common atop the high plateaus of Zion, and the plant community found here is well adapted to periodic burns.

The first views of the hike are northward, and they feature the lofty Pink Cliffs of the Virgin Rim, which rise to 10,000 feet along the northern horizon. These cliffs are made up of freshwater limestone that is colored by oxides of iron

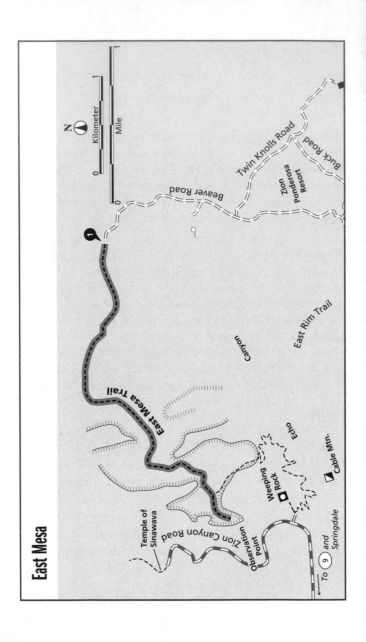

East Mesa

N

Kilometer

Mile

Beaver Road

Twin Knolls Road

Buck Road

Zion Ponderosa Resort

East Rim Trail

Canyon

East Mesa Trail

Temple of Sinawava

Zion Canyon Road

Observation Point

Weeping Rock

Echo

Cable Mtn.

To 9 and Springdale

and manganese. Below them is the Gray Cliffs band, an older layer made of shale deposited in a marine environment.

After 1.5 miles the trail approaches a low knoll. Side paths diverging to the right are bound for overlooks of Mystery Canyon. The White Cliffs found in this canyon are of the same Navajo sandstone that makes up the walls of Zion Canyon. This formation, even more ancient than the marine shales of the Gray Cliffs, was laid down as windblown sand dunes during the Jurassic Period.

The main trail soon swings southwest, revealing views of Echo Canyon as well as the lower reaches of Zion Canyon itself. The West Temple rises prominently above its rim, capped with a thin band of reddish limestone. The trail strikes the south rim of a nameless cleft that joins the Virgin River just below The Narrows, and this overlook offers excellent views of the White Cliffs. Upon crossing a low saddle, the trail passes several sandy camp spots, then makes a brief descent to meet the Observation Point Trail 0.2 mile from its terminus.

Turn right onto the Observation Point Trail. A level trek through deep sand leads to the tip of the promontory and an inspiring view down Zion Canyon. The Great White Throne looms to the south, and to the left the cableworks atop Cable Mountain can be picked out with binoculars. Perhaps the most intriguing feature that can be seen from here is Red Arch Mountain. A great slab of stone broke away from its face in the 1880s, leaving a lofty alcove reminiscent of a cathedral nave. Views to the north are obscured by a shoulder of chalky sandstone, but some of the reddish pinnacles that guard the Temple of Sinawava can be seen from the western edge of the point.

Miles and Directions

0.0 Start at East Mesa trailhead.

3.0 Reach junction with Observation Point Trail. Bear right.

4.0 Arrive at Observation Point.

8.0 Arrive back at the trailhead.

2 Canyon Overlook

A short out-and-back day hike to an overlook of lower Zion Canyon.

Distance: 1.0 mile (1.6 km) round-trip

Approximate hiking time: 30 minutes

Best season: March through November

Difficulty: Moderate

Water availability: None

Hazards: Cliff exposure

Topo maps: Springdale East; *Zion National Park* (ZNHA)

Jurisdiction: Zion National Park (See Appendix A for more information.)

Finding the trailhead: From the Zion Visitor Center, drive east on Utah Highway 9 for 5 miles. The trailhead is just beyond the first tunnel.

The Hike

This short but scenic trail runs to a high overlook immediately above the Great Arch, commanding vistas of the lower reaches of Zion Canyon. Interpretive brochures found at the trailhead explain the plants, animals, and geological features found along the route.

The path initially climbs a series of stairsteps, then traverses

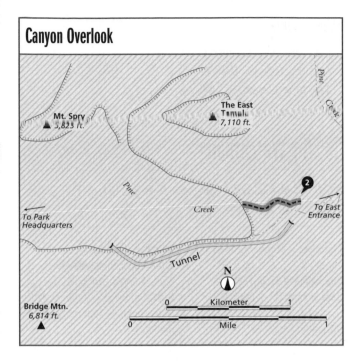

Canyon Overlook

Mt. Spry
5,823 ft.

The East
Temple
7,110 ft.

Pine
Creek

Pine

Creek

To Park
Headquarters

To East
Entrance

Tunnel

N

Bridge Mtn.
6,814 ft.

0   Kilometer   1

0   Mile   1

across the upper walls of the deep slot canyon of Pine Creek. The path passes beneath several overhangs, and in a few spots offers uneven footing above drop-offs; proceed with caution. The path ultimately emerges onto a hilltop covered with hoodoos, or pillars of eroded stone. It then weaves across the slickrock and between piñon pines to reach a spectacular vista point. East Temple looms to the north, while to the west spreads a panorama highlighted by Bridge Mountain, the West Temple, the Towers of the Virgin, and the Streaked Wall. Travelers carrying binoculars can scan the cliffs to the south for desert bighorn sheep, which have been reintroduced into Zion National Park.

Miles and Directions

   0.0   Start at the trailhead on UT 9.

   0.5   Reach Canyon Overlook.

   1.0   Arrive back at the trailhead.

3 The Watchman

An out-and-back hike into the foothills below The Watchman and Bridge Mountain.

Distance: 2.0 miles (3.2 km) round-trip
Approximate hiking time: 1 hour
Best season: April through October
Difficulty: Easy

Water availability: None
Topo maps: Springdale East; *Zion National Park* (ZNHA)
Jurisdiction: Zion National Park (See Appendix A for more information.)

Finding the trailhead: Head north from Zion National Park's South Entrance and take the first right toward The Watchman Campground. In the campground take the first left and park in the area provided at The Watchman trailhead.

The Hike

Climbing into the foothills beneath Bridge Mountain and The Watchman, this short trail begins on a set of wooden steps leading northward up a small knoll. Stay on the main trail, avoiding side trails created by a large population of mule deer. The official trail is about 3 feet wide and traverses the base of the first knoll toward the National Park Service

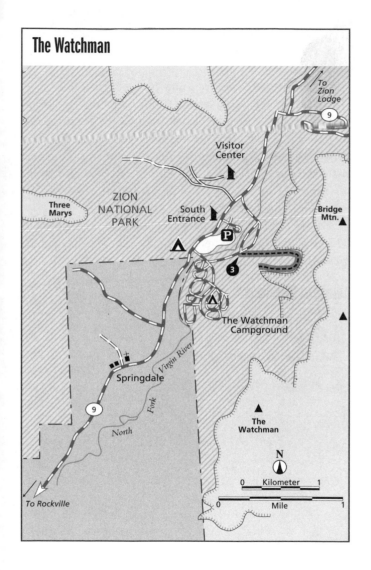

The Watchman

To Zion Lodge

9

Visitor Center

Three Marys

ZION NATIONAL PARK

South Entrance

Bridge Mtn.

P

3

The Watchman Campground

Virgin River

Springdale

North Fork

9

The Watchman

To Rockville

N

0 Kilometer 1

0 Mile 1

residential areas. The vegetation in this area is characterized by a scrub woodland of juniper and piñon pine with sagebrush in the sunny openings.

The path then turns east and proceeds up the base of Bridge Mountain via a series of long switchbacks. Hikers will view overhanging cliffs and stratified rock layers along the trail as they ascend across the stone walls. In addition to views of Bridge Mountain and The Watchman throughout the hike, travelers can look westward across the Virgin River for a fine vista of the Towers of the Virgin and south toward the town of Springdale.

At the top of this trail, a loop path crowns the foothill. This short loop provides several good perches from which to view the surrounding geological wonders.

Miles and Directions

0.0 Start at the trailhead.
1.0 Reach The Watchman viewpoint.
2.0 Arrive back at the trailhead.

4 West Bank of the Virgin River

A day hike along the Virgin River, from the Court of the Patriarchs viewpoint to the Grotto trailhead.

Distance: 5.2 miles (8.4 km) round-trip
Approximate hiking time: 2 hours, 30 minutes
Best season: Year-round
Difficulty: Easy
Water availability: The Virgin River always has water, but it is silty.

Topo maps: Springdale East, Temple of Sinawava; *Zion National Park* (ZNHA)
Jurisdiction: Zion National Park (See Appendix A for more information.)

Finding the trailhead: The trail begins at the Court of the Patriarchs viewpoint, 2.2 miles up Zion Canyon Road (take the tram). It ends at the Grotto trailhead, at Mile 3.2 on Zion Canyon Road.

The Hike

Following trails along the west bank of the Virgin River, this short hike provides an alternative to the scenic drive for visitors who prefer to experience nature outside their cars. The trail is level and easy, but it is heavily traveled by horse parties between the Emerald Pools trailhead and the Court of the Patriarchs. Nonstop views of Zion Canyon are found all along the route, and the lowlands along the river are excellent places to spot birds and, in twilight hours, mule deer.

From the Court of the Patriarchs viewpoint, follow the service road west past a large water tank to reach a bridge over the Virgin River. After crossing the bridge, turn left and

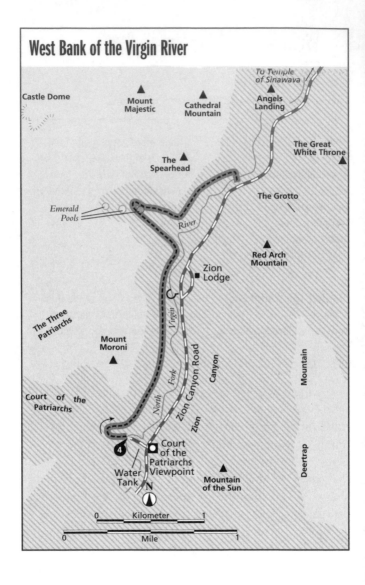

West Bank of the Virgin River

To Temple of Sinawava

Castle Dome

▲ Mount Majestic

▲ Cathedral Mountain

Angels Landing

▲ The Great White Throne

The Spearhead ▲

The Grotto

Emerald Pools

River

▲ Red Arch Mountain

■ Zion Lodge

The Three Patriarchs

Virgin

▲ Mount Moroni

Zion Canyon Road

Court of the Patriarchs

North Fork

Zion Canyon

Mountain

Deertrap

④ Court of the Patriarchs Viewpoint

Water Tank

N

▲ Mountain of the Sun

0   Kilometer   1

0   Mile   1

follow the trail into the center of the Court of the Patri-
archs. Views are stunning beneath the giant monoliths of
Navajo sandstone that line this deep alcove in the wall of
Zion Canyon.

Continuing on, hikers will reach an unmarked trail junction at the edge of a grassy hill; turn right as the path climbs
to an arid knoll and passes the remains of an old corral. The
trail levels off here and follows the river northward. Due to
the gradient of the river, hikers will reach the river bottoms
without any noticeable loss of altitude. The bottomlands are
robed in a riparian woodland of cottonwood and box elder.
Mule deer often appear on the far bank of the river during
the twilight hours. This is also the habitat of the elusive ring-
tailed cat, which hides beneath rock overhangs by day and
ventures forth to forage at night.

The trail follows the river upward as the bleached sum-
mits of Mount Majestic and Cathedral Mountain rise
beyond the reddish spire called The Spearhead. After a corral across the river marks an end to the horse traffic, a bridge
spans the river, allowing hikers access to the Emerald Pools
trailhead for an early, alternate end to the hike. The trail
ahead now becomes wide and paved. Foot traffic is heavy as
the route climbs steadily before dipping into the stone
amphitheater that bears the Emerald Pools. Spur trails climb
to the upper pools, while the main trail runs around the
edge of Lower Emerald Pool, with its rock overhang, delicate waterfalls, and hanging gardens. To continue the trek,
bear right and follow signs for The Grotto trailhead as the
trail threads its way through these picturesque rock gardens
to reach a fine viewpoint at the bowl's edge.

The path then traverses northward, staying above a low
cliff of Springdale sandstone. The Great White Throne

presents its alabaster profile above the far bank of the river as the trail covers the final distance to a bridge that leads to The Grotto trailhead.

Miles and Directions

0.0 Start at the Court of the Patriarchs viewpoint. Follow the service road to the river.

0.1 Cross a footbridge over the North Fork of the Virgin River.

0.3 At the trail junction, turn right for West Bank Trail.

1.3 Reach a horse ford to corrals on the east bank of the river. The trail to Middle and Upper Emerald Pools climbs to left. Keep going straight.

1.4 Reach a footbridge with access to Zion Lodge.

1.9 Arrive at Lower Emerald Pool.

2.0 Reach junction with trail to upper pools. Bear right.

2.6 Reach junction with Angels Landing–West Rim Trail. Cross bridge to finish the hike at The Grotto trailhead.

5.2 Arrive back at the trailhead.

5 Emerald Pools

A network of trails of varied lengths to the Lower, Middle, and Upper Emerald Pools.

Distance: 1.2 to 2.6 miles (1.9 to 4.0 km) round-trip
Approximate hiking time: 45 minutes to 1 hour, 30 minutes
Best season: March through November
Difficulty: Easy (Lower and Middle Pools); moderate (Upper Pool)

Water availability: Emerald Pools have a permanent supply of water, but hikers are asked to bring their own drinking water.
Topo maps: Temple of Sinawava; *Zion National Park* (ZNHA)
Jurisdiction: Zion National Park (See Appendix A for more information.)

Finding the trailhead: From the Zion Visitor Center, take the Zion Canyon tram to Zion Lodge. The trailhead and parking area are on the west side of the road opposite the lodge.

The Hike

There are three Emerald Pools—Upper, Middle, and Lower—and visitors may choose from as many trails: a 1.2-mile out-and-back hike to the Lower Pool; a 1.9-mile round-trip loop to the Middle and Lower Pools; or a 2.6-mile round-trip hike to all three. The paths to the Lower and Middle Pools are wide sidewalks and easily traveled. The Lower Pool is accessible to people in wheelchairs if they have assistance. The trail from the Middle Pool to the Upper Pool is more difficult. This path is no longer maintained and is classified by the National Park Service as strenuous, with its uneven sand and rock surface and moderate to strenuous grade.

Emerald Pools

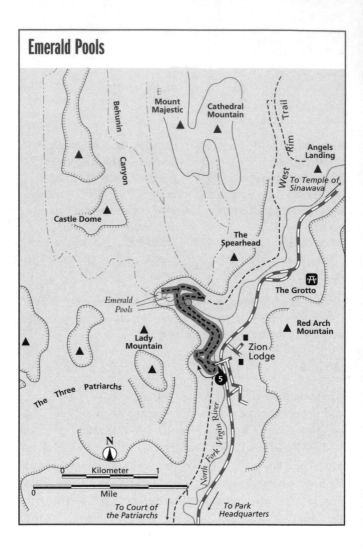

Behunin Canyon

Mount Majestic

Cathedral Mountain

West Rim Trail

Angels Landing

To Temple of Sinawava

Castle Dome

The Spearhead

The Grotto

Emerald Pools

Lady Mountain

Red Arch Mountain

Zion Lodge

5

The Three Patriarchs

N

North Fork Virgin River

0   Kilometer   1

0   Mile   1

To Court of the Patriarchs

To Park Headquarters

While visiting these pools, refrain from bathing in or walking through the water.

From the parking area, cross the bridge to the west side of the Virgin River, where a trailhead sign is located. Hikers who wish to travel directly to the Lower Pool can take the sidewalk to the right. Those wishing to visit the Middle and Upper Pools should follow the path that climbs to the left. The trail description here follows the rocky path that climbs toward the Middle and Upper Pools.

The trail briefly parallels the Virgin River. The Middle Pool trail soon doglegs to the right and heads up a mild grade. Portions of the path have been paved with concrete. The trail up to the Middle Pool is lined with box elder, juniper, bigtooth maple, and Gambel oak. As it progresses up the slope, the trail presents views of formations such as Lady Mountain, The Spearhead, Mount Majestic, Red Arch Mountain, Deertrap Mountain, and the Great White Throne rising above Zion Canyon.

The Middle Pool occupies a large, open area surrounded by slickrock. Pools of water have collected from the trickles above. At the edge of the main pool is a long drop-off leading down to Lower Emerald Pool. From this vantage point, visitors can look out over canyon bottoms filled with a lush deciduous forest.

Traverse across the Middle Pools area to find a small trailhead sign that marks a narrow path to the Upper Pool. This 0.3-mile trail is no longer maintained by the park staff. The trail is uneven and rocky and climbs up a moderately strenuous grade. The Upper Pool itself is surrounded on three sides by sheer cliffs and closed in on the fourth side by a boulder foothill. Maple trees shade this natural amphitheater, making this one of the most peaceful day-hike destinations in Zion Canyon.

To get from the Middle Pool down to the Lower Pool, follow the well-worn path to the north. This trail turns east and splits: The higher trail runs toward the Grotto picnic area, while the lower path heads to Lower Emerald Pool. The trail to Lower Emerald Pool descends quickly along stone steps peppered with sand. Looking down toward the pool, visitors will see a large alcove with a fine veil of water dripping over its edge and into a large mirror surrounded by Gambel oak, maple, and box elder. Follow the trail as it winds beneath the alcove past the pool before returning to the trailhead on the far bank of the Virgin River.

Miles and Directions

0.0 Start at the trailhead for Lower and Middle Pools. Turn left to begin loop trip.

0.9 Arrive at Middle Emerald Pool; junction with trail to Upper Emerald Pool (0.3 mile, moderately strenuous).

1.2 Reach junction with trail to Lower Emerald Pool and trail to Grotto Picnic Area. Turn right to visit the lower pool and return to the trailhead.

1.3 Reach Lower Emerald Pool.

1.9 Arrive back at the trailhead.

6 Angels Landing

An out-and-back day hike to the summit of Angels Landing.

Distance: 4.4 miles (7 km) round-trip
Approximate hiking time: 2 hours, 15 minutes
Best season: March through November
Difficulty: Moderately strenuous
Water availability: The Virgin River always has water, but it is silty.
Hazards: Cliff exposure
Topo maps: Temple of Sinawava; *Zion National Park* (ZNHA)
Jurisdiction: Zion National Park (See Appendix A for more information.)

Finding the trailhead: The trail begins at The Grotto trailhead, 0.6 mile beyond Zion Lodge on Zion Canyon Road (accessed via the tram).

The Hike

This trail offers a spectacular day trip to well-conditioned hikers who have no fear of heights. It receives heavy use, so chances for solitude are slim. Beyond Scout Lookout, the trail becomes an uneven route across sheer cliffs, with chains bolted into the rock face to serve as handrails. This part of the route can be extremely slippery and dangerous when wet or icy and should be avoided unless dry conditions can be depended upon. It is not a good place to take young children in any weather.

The trail begins by crossing a bridge over the Virgin River, then turns north at a junction with the Emerald Pools Trail. Following the river, the path passes through a riparian woodland of cottonwood and box elder, with canyon grape

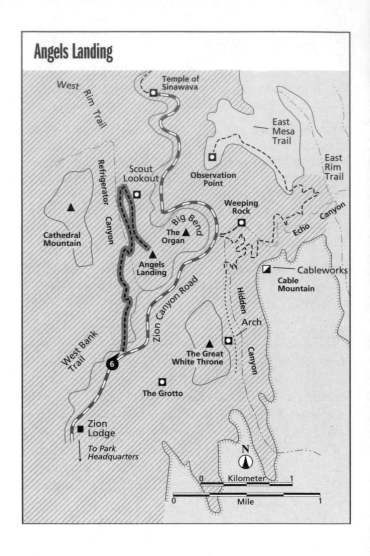

Angels Landing

West Rim Trail

Temple of
Sinawava

East
Mesa
Trail

East
Rim
Trail

Refrigerator Canyon

Scout
Lookout

Observation
Point

Weeping
Rock

Echo Canyon

Cathedral
Mountain

Big Bend

The Organ

Angels
Landing

Cableworks

Cable
Mountain

Zion Canyon Road

Hidden

Arch

Canyon

West Bank Trail

6

The Great
White Throne

The Grotto

Zion
Lodge

To Park
Headquarters

N

0   Kilometer   1

0   Mile   1

and tamarisk growing in the understory. Angels Landing looms ahead, with the mouth of Refrigerator Canyon tucked between this monolith and the west wall of Zion Canyon.

The trail climbs vigorously to reach the elevated mouth of Refrigerator Canyon, then levels off as it enters the cool inner recesses of the cleft. Cool-climate plants such as bigtooth maple and white fir thrive in the shade of the canyon floor, and the vertical walls of red sandstone are pocked with grottos and overhangs.

As the path nears the head of the canyon, it begins a strenuous ascent of the east wall. A series of twenty-one switchbacks has been built cunningly into a rift in the wall here and bears the traveler upward at a calf-burning pace. Known as "Walter's Wiggles," these carefully crafted stoneworks are regarded as one of the engineering marvels of the park. Soon after reaching the top of the switchbacks, the path makes a gradual ascent to a sandy pad called Scout Lookout. It occupies the saddle behind Angels Landing, offering aerial views into Zion Canyon for travelers who lack the stomach for the final and hair-raising pitch to the top of Angels Landing.

The West Rim Trail climbs northwest from Scout Lookout, while the Angels Landing Trail bears southeast. It follows the spine of a knife-edge ridge, with heavy chains attached to the rock to serve as handrails along most (but not all) of the drop-offs. Hikers must make a steep scramble to surmount the first knob, followed by an unprotected walk across a narrow saddle that is flanked by sheer drop-offs. One truly gets a feeling of walking on the razor's edge here. Climbing then resumes, aided by more handrails and footholds hewn into bedrock. This is the long and final pitch to the summit.

There are no guardrails on Angels Landing, where gnarled piñon pines grow from impossible toeholds above the dizzying void. Occupying the center of the Big Bend of Zion Canyon, the summit commands a spectacular 360-degree panorama of rugged spires and towering walls. Highlights include the Great White Throne, Red Arch Mountain, and the entrance to The Narrows.

Miles and Directions

0.0 Start at The Grotto trailhead.

0.1 Cross a footbridge over North Fork of Virgin River and reach junction with West Bank Trail. Turn right for Angels Landing.

1.1 Trail enters Refrigerator Canyon.

1.8 Reach junction with West Rim Trail at Scout Lookout. Turn right for the summit of Angels Landing. Footing becomes treacherous.

2.2 Reach Angels Landing summit.

4.4 Arrive back at the trailhead.

7 Temple of Sinawava

A short out-and-back trip from the parking lot to the "temple."

Distance: 2.0 miles (3.2 km) round-trip
Approximate hiking time: 1 hour
Best season: June through July, September through October
Difficulty: Easy
Water availability: The Virgin River carries a permanent flow of water, although the river is quite silty.
Hazards: Flash-flood danger
Topo maps: Temple of Sinawava; *Zion National Park* (ZNHA)
Jurisdiction: Zion National Park (See Appendix A for more information.)

Finding the trailhead: The trail begins at the Temple of Sinawava parking area at the end of Zion Canyon Road, accessed via the tram.

The Hike

The hike begins on a paved walkway that departs from the Temple of Sinawava parking area. It ends at the mouth of The Narrows, where the canyon constricts around the river and wading is required for further progress up the canyon.

The "temple" is a wide spot in the canyon. Frederick Vining Fisher, a Methodist Minister, explored the area in 1916 and gave religious names to many of the scenic features, including the Great White Throne and Angels Landing. The temple has been the site of many weddings over the years.

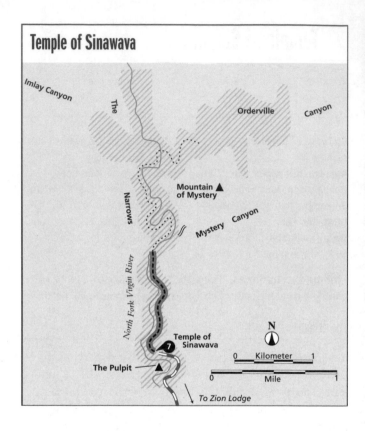

Temple of Sinawava

Imlay Canyon

The

Orderville

Canyon

Mountain ▲
of Mystery

Narrows

Mystery Canyon

North Fork Virgin River

Temple of
Sinawava

7

The Pulpit ▲

N

0   Kilometer   1

0   Mile   1

To Zion Lodge

Miles and Directions

0.0   Start at the Temple of Sinawava trailhead.

1.0   Reach the mouth of The Narrows.

2.0   Arrive back at trailhead.

8 Eagle Crags

An out-and-back climb to the foot of Eagle Crags in the Vermilion Cliffs.

Distance: 6.2 miles (9.6 km) round-trip

Approximate hiking time: 3 hours

Best season: March through May, September through November

Difficulty: Moderately strenuous

Water availability: None

Hazards: Unstable footing on steep, rocky slopes

Topo maps: Springdale West, Smithsonian Butte; *Zion National Park* (ZNHA)

Jurisdiction: Bureau of Land Management, St. George Field Office (See Appendix A for more information.)

Finding the trailhead: From the South Entrance of Zion National Park, drive 4.7 miles west on Utah Highway 9 to Rockville. Head south (left) on Grafton Road and go 0.3 mile to Bridge Road, an unimproved road. Bridge Road has an uneven surface and traverses up steep slopes with few places to turn around. A high-clearance vehicle is recommended from this point on. Several private residences are located at the top of the hill. When the road splits into three branches, continue up the middle road. After 1.4 miles look for a trailhead sign and pullout area on the right.

The Hike

This moderately strenuous hike has both gradual and steep changes in elevation. The trail surface is uneven and rocky in most areas, with the exception of some areas east and south of the crags, which are predominantly sand. The trail itself travels across land managed by the Bureau of Land Management to reach the foot of Eagle Crags, a series of knifelike pinna-

Eagle Crags

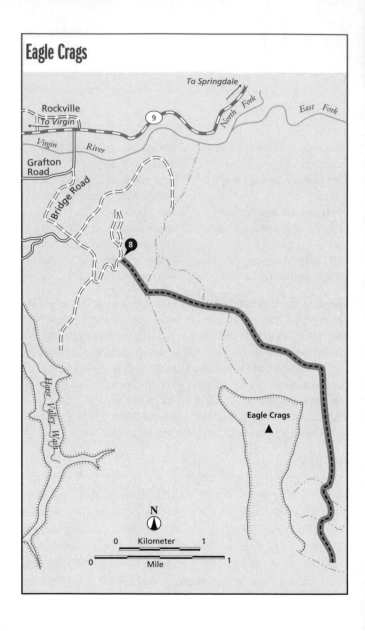

To Springdale

North Fork

East Fork

Rockville

To Virgin

9

Virgin River

Grafton Road

Bridge Road

8

Horse Valley Wash

Eagle Crags ▲

N

0   Kilometer   1

0   Mile   1

cles rising from a lone butte. It then climbs a series of switchbacks to provide closer views of the towering spires.

From the trailhead, follow the path to the right of the trailhead sign and head down a slope to the south. The trail is predominantly sandy, rocky, and uneven and is used heavily by horse parties. If you encounter horses on the trail, step aside and yield the right-of-way. Early on the trail, hikers can see the Eagle Crags to the south and Shunesburg Mountain to the east.

The trail continues downhill until it crosses a draw and ascends the opposite foothill on a southeasterly heading. During this ascent, visitors will encounter a hiker gate through a barbed-wire fence. Pass through the gate and continue to climb southeast across the foothills of the crags. Along the way are eastward views of the Vermilion Cliffs and South Mountain.

After eventually turning down into a draw and traversing another wash, the path turns east and parallels the wash as it makes its way around the base of the foothill to the right (south). The trail then approaches a confluence and turns south, staying on the west side and paralleling the contributing wash. The trail crosses the wash and continues southeast.

Views of Eagle Crags are sometimes hidden by the foothills as the trail winds around to the northeast side of the formation. The trail soon emerges onto an open slope, however, and begins to ascend below the east side of the crags. This slope offers uninterrupted views of Shunesburg Mountain, the Vermilion Cliffs, and South Creek.

At the top of the slope, the trail turns right and heads up to the crags via a series of switchbacks. This is a moderate climb over an uneven, rocky path. At the foot of the crags, the trail straightens out and briefly levels off. The quite narrow path then begins to climb across a steep slope—watch your footing. At the end of this slope, the trail passes a large, flat, overhanging rock from which junipers are growing. After more climbing, hikers reach the crest of the foothill and the eastern end of the crag formations.

Looking up at the spires, travelers will see the reason for the name Eagle Crags. Enjoy the fine views across the valley to the east before you head back along the same route from this great turnaround spot.

Hikers can follow the upward path a short distance to its very end as it wraps around to the south side of the crags. Staying in the upland areas, the route passes over two draws. The path across the draws is narrow and uneven, with loose rocks and steep slopes. Use careful footing along this stretch. Beyond the draws the path gradually loses elevation. As it heads down toward the head of South Creek, the trail abruptly ends in a series of small runoff washes. Another path leads down a very steep slope into a large draw, but it ends abruptly on the other side.

Miles and Directions

- **0.0** Start at the BLM trailhead sign.
- **3.1** The trail ends below Eagle Crags.
- **6.2** Arrive back at the trailhead.

9 Northgate Peaks

A short day hike to an overlook between the Northgate Peaks.

Distance: 4.4 miles (7.0 km) round-trip
Approximate hiking time: 2 hours, 30 minutes
Best season: May through October
Difficulty: Easy

Water availability: A seep east of Pocket Mesa is intermittent
Topo map: *Zion National Park* (ZNHA)
Jurisdiction: Zion National Park (See Appendix A for more information.)

Finding the trailhead: From the town of Virgin, follow the paved Kolob Reservoir Road northward. The road crosses the boundary of Zion National Park three times on its way to the Wildcat Canyon trailhead at Mile 16. The hike begins at this misnamed trailhead.

The Hike

The trek begins in the shadow of Pine Valley Peak, a lone pinnacle of bone-white Navajo sandstone. The path heads eastward across open sage meadows; soon a sprinkling of pines rises to either side. Upon approaching the compact mass of Pocket Mesa, the path veers southward and the pines coalesce into a gladed woodland.

In the midst of the savannah, the trail reaches a junction with the Wildcat Canyon Connector Trail; turn left here. After an eastward jog of 0.1 mile, you'll see a signpost marking the spot where the Northgate Peaks Trail breaks away to the south. Turn right and follow the path to the top of a rise, where a well-beaten spur splits to the left en route to an

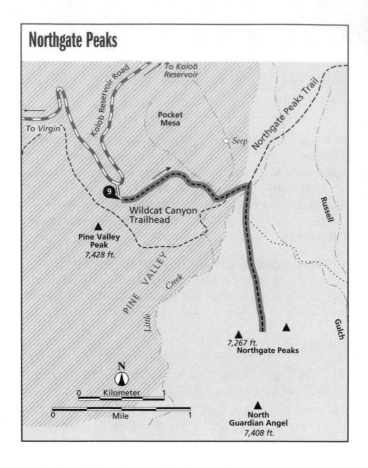

Northgate Peaks

To Kolob
Reservoir

Kolob Reservoir Road

To Virgin

Pocket
Mesa

Seep

Northgate Peaks Trail

9

Wildcat Canyon
Trailhead

Pine Valley
Peak
7,428 ft.

PINE VALLEY

Little Creek

Russell

Gulch

7,267 ft.
Northgate Peaks

N

0 — Kilometer — 1

0 — Mile — 1

**North
Guardian Angel**
7,408 ft.

overlook of the white cliffs of Russell Gulch and onward into the canyon of the Left Fork. The main trail continues straight ahead, following the crest of a promontory that is cloaked in copses of pine and grassy meadows. This path runs out onto a lava outcrop presenting a spectacular view of the Northgate Peaks and North Guardian Angel.

Miles and Directions

0.0 Start at the Wildcat Canyon trailhead.

0.9 Reach junction with Wildcat Canyon Connector. Turn left.

1.0 Reach junction with Northgate Peaks Trail. Turn right (south).

2.2 Arrive at the Northgate Peaks overlook.

4.4 Arrive back at the trailhead.

10 Middle Fork of Taylor Creek

A trail along the Middle Fork of Taylor Creek, ending at Double Arch Alcove.

Distance: 5.0 miles (8.0 km) round-trip
Approximate hiking time: 2 hours, 30 minutes
Best season: March through November
Difficulty: Easy

Water availability: Reliable
Topo maps: Kolob Arch; *Zion National Park* (ZNHA)
Jurisdiction: Zion National Park (See Appendix A for more information.)

Finding the trailhead: Follow Interstate 15 to the Kolob Canyon Visitor Center. From the visitor center drive 2 miles east along the park road to a parking area on the left (north) side of the road. Look for the trailhead sign on the east side of the parking lot.

The Hike

This easy trail takes hikers up the canyon of the Middle Fork of Taylor Creek to two historic homestead cabins and Double Arch Alcove. An alcove is a "blind" arch formed in a rock face through which there are no gaps for daylight to pass. In

Middle Fork of Taylor Creek

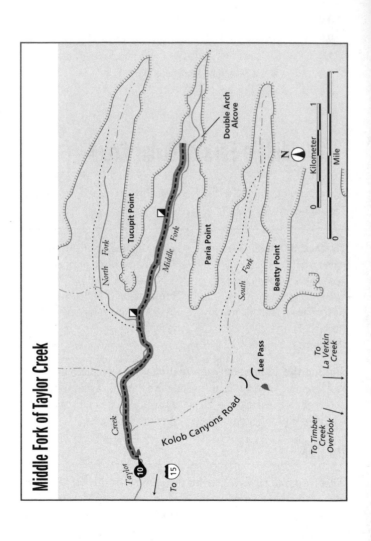

Taylor Creek

10

15 To

Kolob Canyons Road

Lee Pass

North Fork

Middle Fork

South Fork

Tucupit Point

Paria Point

Beatty Point

Double Arch Alcove

To Timber Creek Overlook

To La Verkin Creek

N

Kilometer

Mile

0 1

addition to Double Arch Alcove, hikers are rewarded with spectacular views of Tucupit Point and Paria Point as they approach the canyon. The creekbed is fairly narrow, so be prepared to get wet at numerous stream crossings.

The trail begins from a sign at the east end of the parking lot. The path immediately descends a set of wooden steps down to the creekbed. The vegetation bordering the creek consists of manzanita, sagebrush, juniper, ponderosa pine, and piñon pine. From the bottom of the staircase, the path turns right and heads upstream toward the mouth of the canyon, with views of Horse Ranch Mountain off to the left (northeast). Portions of the trail are sandy and may offer difficult traveling after rains.

The path is easy to follow as it crisscrosses the watercourse several times. Beyond the sixth crossing, hikers may confuse the path with other social trails in the area. The main trail departs from the north bank of the stream, crosses a small island, then picks up again on the south bank. As streamside benches begin to narrow, travel along the trail becomes a bit more difficult. The trail climbs up and out of the stream bottoms several times.

After a mile the trail reaches the confluence of the North and Middle Forks. Look for a trail sign and the Larson homestead cabin in this area. Gustav Larson built the cabin in 1930 from white fir logs hauled in by wagon from Cedar City. He spent summers here from 1930 to 1933, homesteading the Kolob area and raising pigs.

Beyond the cabin the trail crosses the North Fork and ascends into the canyon between Tucupit and Paria Points. Once inside the canyon, the trail stays low along the creekbed. A second homestead cabin can be found about three-quarters of the way up the canyon on a bench above the north bank of the creek. Arthur Fife built this cabin from white fir logs in 1930. Fife was a teacher at Southern Utah State College, now Southern Utah University. When not teaching, he spent his time at the cabin raising goats.

As hikers near the end of the trail, the path climbs onto the south bench to bypass a fallen tree lying in the creekbed. The trail ends at Double Arch Alcove, with its spectacular streaked overhang that encloses a shady pocket.

Miles and Directions

0.0 Start at the trailhead.

1.0 Reach the confluence of North and Middle Forks of Taylor Creek.

2.5 The trail ends at Double Arch Alcove.

5.0 Return to the trailhead.

Cedar Breaks and
Markagunt High Country

The Markagunt Plateau is one of the loftiest uplands in western Utah. The Paiute gave the plateau its name, which means "Highland of Trees." Indeed, a rich forest of subalpine fir and spruce graces the rolling surface of the plateau, interspersed with broad, grassy meadows where elk and mule deer come to graze. Bristlecone pines cling to the windy precipices on the rims of the plateau, surviving extremes of cold and drought.

Because of the plateau's high elevation, hiking opportunities are limited to the summer months. The deep snowdrifts of winter often linger until June, and autumn snows force road closures as early as October. Cool summer temperatures atop the Markagunt make it a haven from the scorching heat found at lower elevations. In winter the area receives enough snow for cross-country skiing. Access to the Markagunt Plateau is via Utah Highway 14, which runs between Cedar City and Long Valley Junction. The highway is plowed free of snow during the wintertime, but only during daylight hours.

The jewel in the crown of the Markagunt Plateau is Cedar Breaks National Monument. This small preserve encompasses a broad amphitheater filled with cliffs banded in orange and red, castellated with craggy spires and natural arches that rival Bryce Canyon in splendor.

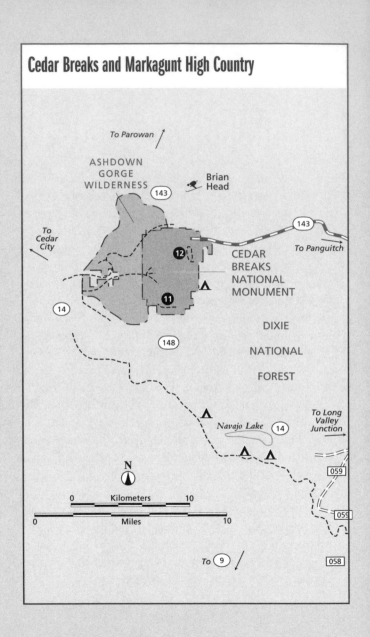

Cedar Breaks and Markagunt High Country

To Parowan

ASHDOWN
GORGE
WILDERNESS

143

Brian
Head

143

To
Cedar
City

To Panguitch

12

CEDAR
BREAKS
NATIONAL
MONUMENT

11

14

148

DIXIE

NATIONAL

FOREST

To Long
Valley
Junction

Navajo Lake   14

059

N

0   Kilometers   10

0   Miles   10

059

To 9

058

11 Ramparts Trail–Spectra Point

A short, out-and-back day hike along the rim of the Cedar Breaks.

Distance: 3.0 miles (5.0 km) round-trip
Approximate hiking time: 1 hour, 30 minutes
Best season: June through September
Difficulty: Moderate
Water availability: The small stream to the west of Spectra Point flows permanently.
Hazards: Cliff exposure, lightning
Topo map: Cedar Breaks National Monument
Jurisdiction: Cedar Breaks National Monument (See Appendix A for more information.)

Finding the trailhead: From Cedar City drive east on Utah Highway 14 for 17.9 miles, then turn north on Utah Highway 148. Follow this road for 3 miles to reach the Cedar Breaks Visitor Center. The Ramparts Trail departs from the west end of the visitor center parking lot.

The Hike

This trail follows the south rim of the Cedar Breaks amphitheater, revealing sweeping vistas of the ragged walls and eroded pinnacles that fill the basin. From the parking lot the path ascends for a short distance to the cliff tops above Jericho Canyon. Here it skirts wind-scoured stands of Englemann spruce and subalpine fir.

Views are spectacular from the outset of the hike, featuring multicolored spires and fins of weathered limestone. As the trail winds in and out of the trees, hikers get southward views of the meadowy top of the Markagunt Plateau.

Ramparts Trail–Spectra Point

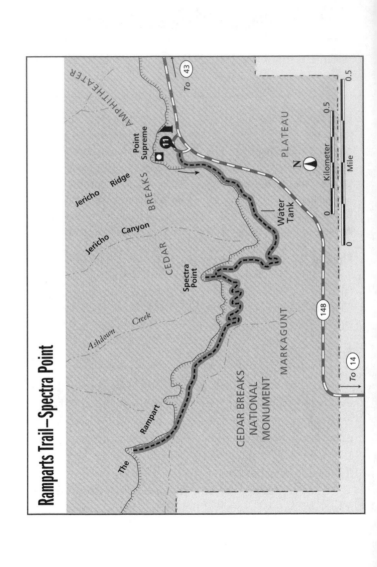

After a mile a spur path runs out to the end of Spectra Point. This long finger of chalky limestone extends northward into the heart of the Cedar Breaks amphitheater. It is one of the finest vantage points for viewing the area's hoodoos and walls, especially during morning and evening, when slanting light illuminates the stone. Prominent features of the badlands include Bristlecone and Chessmen Ridges, which rise from the center of the amphitheater, castellated with tortured pinnacles of all descriptions.

Growing from the arid soils of Spectra Point are hardy specimens of bristlecone pine, twisted by winter gales and splintered by summer lightning storms. The oldest specimen on the point is more than 1,600 years old.

The main trail departs westward from Spectra Point, zigzagging downward into a wooded glen occupied by a crystal-clear rivulet. Spruce, fir, and limber pine tower overhead, shading luxuriant swards of grasses and wildflowers that include lupine, aster, bluebells, and larkspur. The trail descends at a steady clip, making occasional forays to the rims for views of the badlands that stretch away below.

The trail ends at a high overlook of The Rampart, which bears a scattered growth of bristlecone pine. From this point, views stretch from the forested floor of the basin all the way to the banded cliffs that rise 2,000 feet all around it.

Miles and Directions

- **0.0** The trail leaves the parking lot.
- **0.8** Reach Spectra Point.
- **1.5** The trail peters out atop The Rampart.
- **3.0** Arrive back at the parking lot.

12 Alpine Pond

A short, out-and-back day hike through wooded country atop the Markagunt Plateau.

Distance: 2.1-mile (3.4 km) loop

Approximate hiking time: 1 hour

Best season: June through September

Difficulty: Moderate

Water availability: Alpine Pond always has water but is ecologically fragile; take water only from the outlet stream below the pond.

Topo map: Cedar Breaks National Monument

Jurisdiction: Cedar Breaks National Monument (See Appendix A for more information.)

Finding the trailhead: The trail departs from the Chessmen Overlook, 1.7 miles beyond the Cedar Breaks Visitor Center on Utah Highway 148. The trail can also be accessed from the Alpine Pond trailhead, 1 mile farther north.

The Hike

This trail forms a loop through the subalpine forest above the east rim of the Cedar Breaks amphitheater. It is a self-guiding nature walk, with pamphlets provided at either trailhead. We describe the trek as a 2.1-mile loop from the Chessmen Overlook, but hikers can also approach the loop from the Alpine Pond trailhead at its north end or choose between several shorter point-to-point hikes.

From the overlook, follow the Lower Trail downward through a forest of stately spruce and fir. A handful of bristlecone pines grow along the rim of the amphitheater, and gaps in the trees allow glimpses of the northern half of

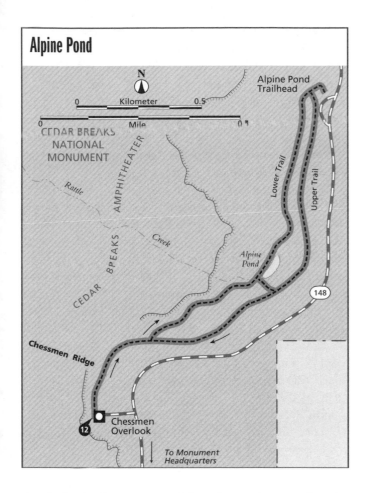

Alpine Pond

N

Kilometer

Mile

Alpine Pond
Trailhead

CEDAR BREAKS
NATIONAL
MONUMENT

Rattle

CEDAR BREAKS AMPHITHEATER

Creek

Lower Trail

Upper Trail

Alpine
Pond

148

Chessmen Ridge

Chessmen
Overlook

12

To Monument
Headquarters

the Cedar Breaks. Less rugged than the southern reaches, the cliffs and spires that appear here are sprinkled with a sparse growth of conifers. The trail follows the rim for almost a mile, then enters a wooded dale that bears the headwaters of Rattle Creek.

The path climbs to the source of the waters, a tiny spring-fed lake known as Alpine Pond. This crystal-clear pool is cupped within a miniature basin surrounded by elegant spires of spruce and fir. It is a favorite watering hole for local wildlife, and it nourishes a vibrant growth of aquatic plants. A connecting path zigzags upward from the foot of the pond to reach the Upper Trail, bisecting the loop and offering shorter hike options for travelers who find themselves pressed for time.

The main trail follows the western shore of the pond, then ascends gradually through a series of pocket meadows. It soon reaches a quarrylike slope of broken rock, known as a talus slope. The loose boulders make an ideal nesting habitat for a variety of rodents. Look for badger-size yellow-bellied marmots; smaller pikas, or "rock rabbits"; and diminutive least chipmunks.

The path soon climbs toward the Alpine Pond trailhead; turn south on the Upper Trail to complete the loop. The trail wends its way through a mature spruce-fir woodland. This forest is an important foraging area for the Douglas squirrel, which harvests cones throughout the summer and hoards them in underground caches for use during the winter months. Some caches are inevitably forgotten, and in favorable conditions the seeds within these lost cones can sprout and help renew the forest.

Numerous snags rise among the living trees in this area, the victims of frequent lightning storms that rage across the high Markagunt Plateau. To local wildlife these trees become even more valuable after they die: They support populations of insects that are a valuable food source and may also become homes for cavity-nesting mammals and birds. Two of the more prevalent cavity-nesting birds found in this area are the flicker and the mountain bluebird.

The trees give way to grassy glades, and sun-loving aspens thrive along the edges of the meadows. Conifers grow in clumps in this area, with skirts of their tiny offspring surrounding them on every side.

After passing the cutoff trail that descends to Alpine Pond, the Upper Trail continues southward along the edge of vast meadows. These meadows offer brilliant displays of wildflowers throughout the summer, highlighted by paintbrush and fleabane. Herds of elk sometimes graze here during autumn. The path ultimately finds its way back to the Chessmen Overlook.

Miles and Directions

0.0 Start at the Chessmen Overlook trailhead.

0.2 The trail splits. Follow Lower Trail, to the left.

0.6 Reach Alpine Pond and junction with cutoff to Upper Trail. Follow Lower Trail around the western shore of the pond.

1.1 Reach junction with short spur to the Alpine Pond trailhead. Turn right onto Upper Trail to complete the loop.

1.5 The cutoff trail descends to Alpine Pond. Bear left.

2.1 The trail ends at Chessmen Overlook.

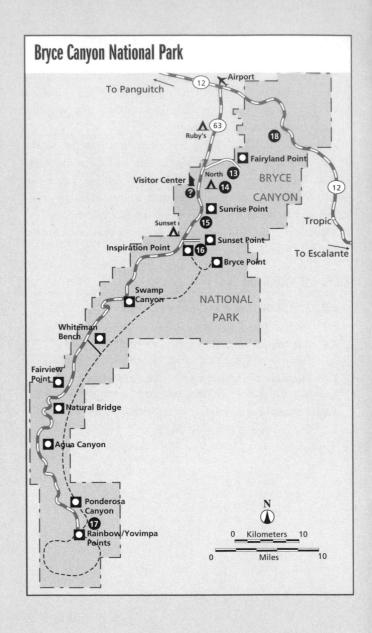

Bryce Canyon National Park

To Panguitch

Airport

12

Ruby's

63

Fairyland Point

Visitor Center

North

13

14

BRYCE

CANYON

12

Sunset

Sunrise Point

15

Tropic

Inspiration Point

16

Sunset Point

To Escalante

Bryce Point

Swamp
Canyon

NATIONAL

PARK

Whiteman
Bench

Fairview
Point

Natural Bridge

Agua Canyon

Ponderosa
Canyon

17

Rainbow/Yovimpa
Points

N

0   Kilometers   10

0   Miles   10

Bryce Canyon National Park

The towering hoodoos, spires, and natural bridges of Bryce Canyon National Park seem to deny all reason or explanation, leaving hikers gazing skyward with jaws agape in wondrous incredulity.

The forces that created Bryce Canyon are still at work today. The bedrock originated sixty million years ago, when southern Utah held a series of low-lying lakebeds. For millions of years, rivers deposited sediments into these lakebeds, eventually filling them and causing the lakes to dry out. The continual deposition of rocks, clays, and silts caused these materials to be compressed and form sedimentary rock layers. Some layers contained deposits of clays and silts, while other layers were rich in lime, dolomite, and carbonates. Throughout all of these layers are iron oxides and manganese compounds, lending hues of orange and purple to the stone. Over time these sediments hardened into rock known as the Claron Formation.

These geologic processes continued unchanged until about sixteen million years ago, when powerful forces began to lift the Colorado Plateau. The stress caused by the uplift created countless joints or vertical cracks throughout the Claron Formation and caused southern Utah to fracture along several fault lines. Resulting from this uplifting force are the nine high plateaus of southern Utah.

Bryce Canyon is not so much a canyon as it is a series of amphitheaters created by erosional forces of the Paria River system along the edge of the Paunsaugunt Plateau. As the streams traveled eastward over the edge and down the slope of the plateau, the waters gained velocity and began to carry away bits of the Claron Formation. As this process continued, gullies cut deeply into the plateau, exposing layers of rock. These gully walls then became vulnerable to other forms of erosion, primarily through trickling water and the freeze-thaw cycle.

Visitors overlooking the canyon rim can see for themselves what time and geological forces have created, and adventurous and curious hikers can take advantage of the park's trails to experience Bryce Canyon on a more intimate level.

Day hikers will find numerous options to suit varying needs. Day hikes through the park range from 1-mile loops to 11-mile round-trip trails. One advantage of hiking in Bryce Canyon is that many of the trails intersect one another and can be connected to form loops. For instance, the Navajo Loop, Peekaboo Loop, and Queens Garden Trails can be combined with short excursions along connecting trails.

Before embarking on any hike in Bryce Canyon National Park, hikers should make sure they carry several essential items. First and foremost is water. Bryce Canyon is extremely hot and dry during summer. Water sources below the rim are severely limited and must be treated prior to consumption. As a rule, always carry ample water to last the duration of the hike, and then some. Carry sunscreen, eye protection, and a hat to prevent overexposure to the sun's rays. Since trails in Bryce Canyon traverse steep and rocky slopes, wear sturdy boots that provide ample support and protection. Always remember that Bryce Canyon sits at a high elevation; lowland visitors must allow themselves time to acclimate to the elevation. Finally, do not overestimate your abilities or overexert yourself while on the trails.

A shuttle runs between the shuttle area outside the park and trails in the main, upper amphitheater, which makes an excellent option to avoid crowded parking lots during busy summer weekends.

Most supplies and services can be found in the nearby town of Panguitch. However, Panguitch is a notorious speed trap: The police have been known to ticket out-of-state visitors traveling below the speed limit. If you don't have Utah license plates, we recommend steering clear.

13 Rim Trail

A popular trail above Bryce Canyon that connects all the scenic overlooks from Fairyland Point to Bryce Point.

Distance: 5.5 miles (8.9 km) point-to-point shuttle
Approximate hiking time: 3 hours
Best season: April through October
Difficulty: Moderate
Water availability: Water is provided at various park restrooms.
Topo maps: Bryce Canyon, Bryce Point; *Trails Illustrated*
Jurisdiction: Bryce Canyon National Park (See Appendix A for more information.)

Finding the trailhead: From the Bryce Canyon Visitor Center, drive north 0.7 mile to the turnoff for Fairyland Point and park in the designated area. From the parking area, walk east to the rim at Fairyland Point and follow the stone path south. The Rim Trail is also accessible from Sunrise, Sunset, Inspiration, and Bryce Points.

The Hike

Note: This point-to-point hike requires a car at both ends of the trail, which can be hiked in either direction.

This very popular path runs along the rim of Fairyland Canyon and Bryce Canyon. Many park visitors hike the Rim Trail since it is accessible from the park road at various lookout points and provides spectacular views of the spires and canyons below. Travelers can choose to hike the entire trail by starting from Fairyland Point or Bryce Point, or break the hike up into smaller segments. Most of the pathway between Sunrise and Inspiration Points is either paved or so well worn that portions are wheelchair accessible.

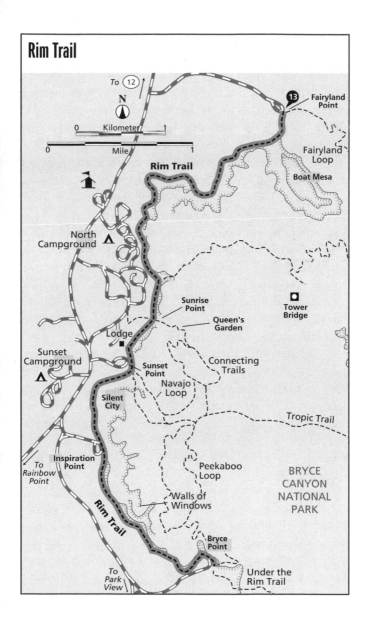

Rim Trail

To (12)

N

0   Kilometer   1
0   Mile   1

Rim Trail

(13) Fairyland
Point

Fairyland
Loop

Boat Mesa

North
Campground

Sunrise
Point

Queen's
Garden

Tower
Bridge

Lodge

Connecting
Trails

Sunset
Campground

Sunset
Point

Navajo
Loop

Silent
City

Tropic Trail

To
Rainbow
Point

Inspiration
Point

Peekaboo
Loop

Walls of
Windows

BRYCE
CANYON
NATIONAL
PARK

Rim Trail

Bryce
Point

Under the
Rim Trail

To
Park
View

However, steep gradients and uneven surfaces may make wheelchair access to some areas difficult.

From Fairyland Point follow the well-worn gravel path southward as it winds upward through a forest of juniper, ponderosa pine, Douglas fir, and bristlecone pine. For about a mile the path intermittently leaves the rim to pass along the westward slopes of hills, blocking views of Fairyland Canyon to the east. The trail emerges into a lightly forested area burned by the Park Service in fall 1995 as a controlled management burn. The path levels off along the rim, then turns southwest into the burn area.

Continuing westward, the trail descends across another slope, moving away from the rim. It eventually winds east to round the hill and emerges once again at the rim of the canyon. Northward views from this location encompass Boat Mesa and the Aquarius Plateau. Bristlecone Point, Canaan Mountain, the Kaiparowits Plateau, and Navajo Mountain can be seen to the east.

From here the path briefly levels out along the rim before ascending westward around another hill. Bristlecone pines grow from the barren, rocky slopes here. The trail eventually starts to descend, looping around to the northeast and again emerging at the canyon rim. From here the trail begins a gradual descent through a dense forest of conifers. The path levels off briefly, then begins to climb along the rim.

Next the path gradually descends toward a junction with the Fairyland Loop. At this junction bear right to continue along the Rim Trail, which traverses an eastward-facing slope that overlooks the canyon. The trail then leaves the slope and descends to Sunrise Point, 0.25 mile south of the Fairyland junction. Views of the Sinking Ship and Boat Mesa present themselves on the final approach to Sunrise Point. As the trail climbs a gradual slope to Sunrise Point, it meets the Queens Garden Trail. Bear right to remain on the Rim Trail. Sunrise Point provides spectacular views of the Bryce Canyon amphitheater below.

Sunset Point is encountered about 0.5 mile south of Sunrise Point. Follow the path as it continues along the rim, providing excellent views of the south rim of Bryce Canyon. A juniper-pine forest with a ground cover of manzanita grows to the west of the trail. Wooden benches at various points along the path give visitors opportunities to relax and enjoy the wondrous scenery.

As the trail nears Sunset Point, northward views once again reveal Boat Mesa, the Sinking Ship, and the Aquarius Plateau. A junction with the Navajo Loop lies just north of Sunset Point. Thor's Hammer lies directly below the rim to the left (north) of the Navajo Loop.

From Sunset Point, visitors can look down to see a small portion of the narrow rift called Wall Street. After taking in the view, follow the paved path southward. The numerous rifts and caverns of the Silent City await, directly below the rim to the south of Sunset Point. Across the canyon the Peekaboo Loop can be seen as it winds around the base of The Cathedral.

The Rim Trail soon meets a spur trail leading to Sunset Campground. Bear left and follow the Rim Trail as it leaves the rim and climbs a moderate grade. Below the trail to the west is a pine forest dominated by ponderosas but including limber pine as well. The trail levels off and quickly returns to the rim with the Silent City to the north and The Cathedral and Wall of Windows to the southeast.

The trail quickly winds around another small hill and

returns to the rim once more before undertaking the steady climb to Inspiration Point and its three overlooks. As the trail approaches the first overlook, the Wall of Windows can be seen to the left (southeast). The northern horizon opens up dramatically as the trail continues to gain elevation. After a steady climb to the second Inspiration Point overlook, hikers can observe the bottom of Bryce Canyon and study the drainage pattern that flows eastward into Bryce Creek. The third Inspiration Point overlook is located on a spur trail at the top of the ascent. From this point one can see the Wall of Windows to the northwest and the town of Tropic in the opposite direction.

Returning along the spur back to the Rim Trail, through-hikers should look for a trail sign that indicates the direction to Bryce Point. The trail now becomes a narrow, unpaved path. The path traverses a ridgeline, passing precariously steep cliffs and crossing a draw. Beyond the draw the narrow path winds up through a pleasant conifer stand. This stretch of trail overlooks the Wall of Windows and grotto formations in the canyon walls. The trail then leaves the rim and begins a gradual descent through a loose growth of conifers. It eventually approaches the rim just above the Wall of Windows and bends southward. Hikers can see more grottos and caverns in the rim wall below Bryce Point, to the southeast.

Once again the trail briefly leaves the rim, then returns to it and descends a series of switchbacks. At the bottom of the grade, the trail levels out and continues a gradual descent until it overlooks a draw. From here it makes a steady climb to Bryce Point. The final approach to Bryce Point is along a steep, westward-facing slope.

Before reaching its terminus at the two Bryce Point

overlooks, the trail meets a spur trail to the Bryce Point parking lot. Turn left to reach the overlooks. These two vantage points provide excellent views northwest into Bryce Canyon, north toward the Aquarius Plateau, and northeast toward the Kaiparowits Plateau.

Miles and Directions

- **0.0** Start at Fairyland Point.
- **2.2** At the junction with Fairyland Loop, bear right.
- **2.5** Reach Sunrise Point.
- **3.0** Reach Sunset Point.
- **3.8** Reach Inspiration Point.
- **4.3** Arrive at Wall of Windows Overlook.
- **5.5** Reach Bryce Point.

14 Queens Garden–Sunrise to Sunset Points

A point-to-point trail descending below the canyon rim.

Distance: 1.4 to 1.5 miles (2.25 to 2.4 km) one-way shuttle

Approximate hiking time: 45 minutes

Best season: April through October

Difficulty: Moderate

Water availability: None

Hazards: Steep slopes, loose gravel

Topo maps: Bryce Canyon, Bryce Point; *Trails Illustrated*

Jurisdiction: Bryce Canyon National Park (See Appendix A for more information.)

Finding the trailhead: From the Bryce Canyon Visitor Center, drive south 0.4 mile to the turnoff for Sunrise Point. Follow road signs to Sunrise Point and park in the designated area. From the parking area, walk southeast along well-worn paths to the Queens Garden trailhead.

The Hike

Note: If you have only one car, you can complete the loop back up to the trailhead at Sunrise Point for an additional 0.7 mile of level hiking above the rims.

The Queens Garden Trail is a short, 0.9-mile route that drops about 320 feet below the canyon rim. Although the trail is not a loop, hikers can loop back up to the rim by combining a connecting trail with either branch of the Navajo Loop. Interesting rock formations along this popular path include Gulliver's Castle, the Queens Castle, and Queen Elizabeth herself.

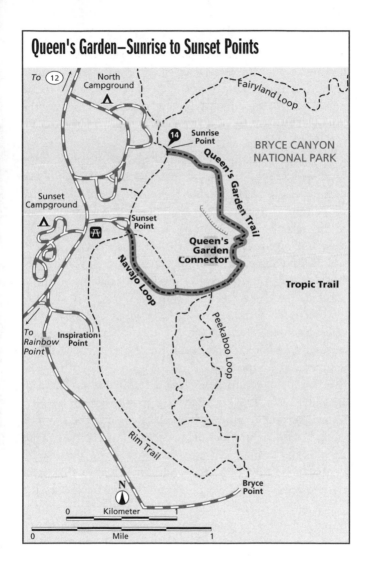

Queen's Garden–Sunrise to Sunset Points

To (12)

North Campground

Fairyland Loop

14 Sunrise Point

BRYCE CANYON NATIONAL PARK

Queen's Garden Trail

Sunset Campground

Sunset Point

Queen's Garden Connector

Navajo Loop

Tropic Trail

To Rainbow Point

Inspiration Point

Peekaboo Loop

Rim Trail

Bryce Point

N

0   Kilometer   1

0   Mile   1

From the trailhead the trail descends along a slope below Sunrise Point. The path briefly traces a ridgeline, but soon returns to a northward-facing slope. Early views include Boat Mesa, the Sinking Ship, and the Aquarius Plateau to the northeast. Bristlecone Point, Canaan Mountain, the Kaiparowits Plateau, and Navajo Mountain show themselves in the east.

The trail continues along this slope until it bends to the south and descends a series of switchbacks. At the bottom of the grade, the path straightens out onto a ridgeline with Bryce Canyon below to the south and a conifer-filled draw to the north. The trail soon descends another set of switchbacks and levels off along a slope with the Aquarius Plateau and the Sinking Ship to the northeast. It then bends right and comes to a junction with the Tropic Trail; bear right to continue the Queens Garden Trail.

The trail continues to descend via a series of short switchbacks to a tunnel cut through a wall of hoodoos. Beyond the tunnel, ragged spires tower over the trail, which continues along the base of the formations, passes between two hoodoos, and again descends via switchbacks. The path straightens out above a draw and passes through another tunnel. Beyond the tunnel the trail bends south and traverses along the slopes overlooking another draw. The trail bends right, passes through a third tunnel, and joins the Navajo Loop Connecting Trail at the bottom of the canyon. Bear right to reach the Navajo Loop, and then turn left onto the western leg of the Navajo Loop. After making a gentle ascent through Wall Street, where two towering Douglas firs have been growing for more than 750 years, the trail ascends along a series of long and short switchbacks before reaching Sunset Point.

Miles and Directions

0.0 Start at the Queens Garden trailhead at Sunrise Point.

0.8 Reach junction with connecting trail to the Navajo Loop. Turn right.

0.9 Junction with the Navajo Loop. Bear left onto the loop's western leg.

1.1 Begin the ascent through Wall Street.

1.5 Arrive at Sunset Point.

15 Navajo Loop

A loop from Sunset Point down to the floor of Bryce Canyon and back again.

Distance: 1.4-mile (2.2 km) loop

Approximate hiking time: 1 to 2 hours

Best season: April through October

Difficulty: Moderate

Water availability: None

Topo maps: Bryce Point; *Trails Illustrated*

Jurisdiction: Bryce Canyon National Park (See Appendix A for more information.)

Finding the trailhead: The trail departs from a signpost at the central overlook point at Sunset Point.

The Hike

This popular trail makes a short one- to two-hour loop from the rim at Sunset Point down to the floor of Bryce Canyon. The trail visits favorite hoodoo formations such as Wall Street, Twin Bridges, and Thor's Hammer.

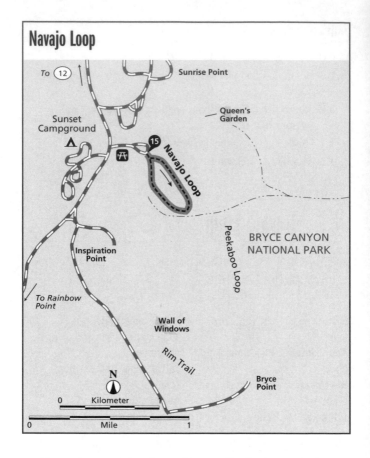

Navajo Loop

To (12)

Sunrise Point

Queen's
Garden

Sunset
Campground

△

⛺

15 Navajo Loop

Inspiration
Point

To Rainbow
Point

Peekaboo Loop

BRYCE CANYON
NATIONAL PARK

Wall of
Windows

Rim Trail

Bryce
Point

N

0 ——— Kilometer

0 ——— Mile ——— 1

From Sunset Point the trail immediately descends along a paved path with safety railings along the edges. After about 100 feet the railing ends and the path splits, with two trails heading off to the right (south) and one trail heading off to the left (east). The left-hand path is the eastern leg of the Navajo Loop; it will be discussed later in this description. The two right-hand paths consist of an upper and a lower trail.

The upper trail is a short spur to a window looking through a hoodoo wall down into the west portion of Bryce Canyon. The lower trail is the first leg of the Navajo Loop; it begins a rapid descent along a series of long and short switchbacks down to the canyon floor. At the bottom of the switchbacks, the trail straightens out and makes a gradual descent through Wall Street, where two towering Douglas firs have been growing in the depths of the rift for more than 750 years.

Upon emerging from Wall Street, hikers follow a wide pathway bordered by manzanita, juniper, and ponderosa pines. The end of the south leg of the Navajo Loop is identified by trail signs for the Peekaboo Loop and Queens Garden Connecting Trails. Hikers can make a hard left turn to complete the remaining 0.6 mile of the Navajo Loop back up to Sunset Point or connect with one of these other paths for a longer hike.

Continuing along the Navajo Loop (the left-hand path noted above), hikers gain enjoyable views of large hoodoo formations flanking both sides of the path. One such formation, Twin Bridges, is located on the right side of the trail at Mile 1.0. Beyond Twin Bridges, the path ascends a series of switchbacks to return to the rim. Look for Thor's Hammer to the north along this final section of trail.

Miles and Directions

0.0   Start at the Navajo Loop trailhead at Sunset Point. Bear right.

0.4   Begin the descent through Wall Street.

0.6   Reach junction with Peekaboo Loop and Queens Garden Connecting Trail. Turn left to complete the Navajo Loop.

1.0   View the Twin Bridges formation on north side of trail.

1.4   The trail returns to Sunset Point.

16 Peekaboo Loop

A loop for hikers and horses through the pink limestone formations below the rim of Bryce Canyon.

Distance: 5.5-mile (8.9 km) loop
Approximate hiking time: 3 hours
Best season: April through October
Difficulty: Moderate
Water availability: None
Topo maps: Bryce Point; *Trails Illustrated*
Jurisdiction: Bryce Canyon National Park (See Appendix A for more information.)

Finding the trailhead: From the Bryce Canyon Visitor Center, drive south 1.6 miles to a turnoff for Inspiration and Bryce Points. Follow road signs to Bryce Point and park in the designated area. The Bryce Point trailhead is at the north corner of the parking lot.

The Hike

A short connector begins at Bryce Point and descends below the rim to connect with the Peekaboo Loop, a hiker and horse trail that winds around hoodoo formations below Inspiration and Bryce Points. Views along this trail include the popular Wall of Windows, The Three Wisemen, The Organ, and The Cathedral, as well as eastward views beyond the canyon toward the Aquarius Plateau, Canaan Mountain, and the Kaiparowits Plateau.

The trail departs from the north corner of the Bryce Point parking lot. From the sidewalk follow the trail as it descends southeast along a slope below the parking lot. The trail soon meets a junction with the Under the Rim

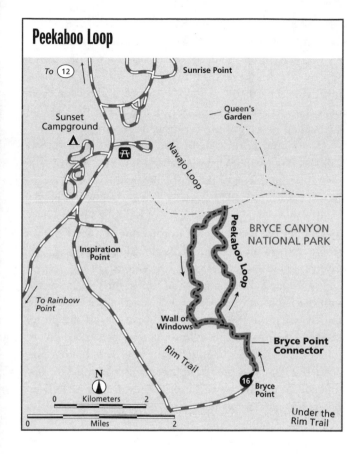

Peekaboo Loop

To (12) ↑

Sunrise Point

Queen's Garden

Sunset Campground ⛺

🏕

Navajo Loop

Peekaboo Loop

BRYCE CANYON
NATIONAL PARK

Inspiration Point

To Rainbow Point ↙

Wall of Windows

Rim Trail

Bryce Point Connector

16 Bryce Point

N
⬆

0   Kilometers   2

0   Miles   2

Under the Rim Trail

Trail; bear right to follow this trail toward The Hat Shop formations.

To reach the Peekaboo Loop, turn left and follow the trail as it descends northeast along a gravel path. Bristlecone and limber pines grow along the trail as it heads down a series of short switchbacks. At the bottom of the grade, the trail straightens out along a slope beneath towering white cliffs of limestone. Northward views here include Bryce Canyon below and Boat Mesa rising in the distance.

The trail drops until it reaches a man-made tunnel. Beyond the tunnel the pathway levels off and continues northwest beneath Bryce Point overlook and several grotto formations. Rockfalls commonly make the path extremely narrow and rocky, making for unstable footing.

Continuing northwest, the trail passes a large hoodoo wall and begins another gradual descent. The Wall of Windows lies to the west of the trail as it turns a switchback and then bends to the right. Hoodoos directly below this portion of the trail provide good examples of resistant, lime-rich layers capping the formation and protecting the weaker layers below from erosion. The trail winds down the slope and traverses beneath these caprock formations.

Just beyond the hoodoos the trail comes to a junction with the Peekaboo Loop. Turn left (west) at the junction to quickly reach the Peekaboo Loop horse corrals and pit toilets. Then turn right and follow the trail as it heads down a switchbacked slope, passing bristlecone and limber pines along the way. The trail straightens and continues to drop gradually along the west side of a draw. Pink hoodoos line the draw's sides as ponderosa pine, juniper, and manzanita grow in the bottom.

The path eventually traverses northwest across the draw and begins a slow ascent across a series of washes, then follows switchbacks up to a tunnel cut into the ridgetop. Beyond the tunnel, the trail bends left and continues up the opposite (north) slope of the ridge. Hoodoos decorate the ridgetops as the trail levels off and winds along the slopes. Other views include Bryce Point and grotto formations to the south of the trail.

The trail eventually makes a short ascent and cuts between two hoodoo formations. At the top of the climb, the rifts and caverns of the Silent City can be seen ahead to the north. The trail begins to descend at the base of The Cathedral. It then straightens out and follows the upper left side of a draw, with Boat Mesa rising on the northern horizon.

Another set of switchbacks drops hikers down into the draw. From here the trail goes down the draw to a junction with the Navajo Loop Connecting Trail. Turn left to return to the Bryce Point trail via the Peekaboo Loop.

The main route heads up a gradual slope here, providing overlooking views of a washbed and the Navajo Loop to the right (west). The path ascends steadily along slopes until it passes through a small cavern. Afterward it levels off somewhat and begins to wind around pink limestone formations above the canyon floor.

After several small ascents and descents, the path passes through a man-made arch and into a small grotto with large hoodoo walls towering above. The trail descends through this cavern via a series of short switchbacks. At the bottom of the switchbacks, it emerges from the cavern with a close-up view of the Wall of Windows to the right. The trail briefly traverses the base of the Wall of Windows. Looking up at the canyon rim from here, hikers can see grottos in the cliffs.

Beyond the Wall of Windows, the trail descends to the canyon floor, where a horse corral and pit toilets are located. The junction with the Bryce Point Trail, which will take you back to your starting point, is located slightly uphill from the horse corral.

Miles and Directions

0.0 Start at the trailhead at Bryce Point.

0.1 At junction with the Under the Rim Trail, turn left.

1.0 At junction with the Peekaboo Loop, turn right.

2.2 At junction with the Navajo Loop Connecting Trail, turn left.

2.5 Arrive at The Cathedral.

3.1 Pass the Wall of Windows.

3.6 Pass the horse corral and pit toilets.

4.0 Return to Bryce Point Trail. Turn right.

5.0 At junction with the Under the Rim Trail, turn right.

5.5 Return to Bryce Point.

17 Bristlecone Loop

A short loop trail above the rim at Rainbow Point.

Distance: 1.0-mile (1.6 km) loop

Approximate hiking time: 30 minutes

Best season: April through October

Difficulty: Easy

Water availability: None

Topo maps: Rainbow Point; *Trails Illustrated*

Jurisdiction: Bryce Canyon National Park (See Appendix A for more information.)

Finding the trailhead: From the Bryce Canyon Visitor Center, drive 16.8 miles south to Rainbow Point. Follow the sidewalk to the southeast side of the parking lot to the Bristlecone Loop trailhead sign. An additional trailhead sign is located to the left of the restrooms.

Bristlecone Loop

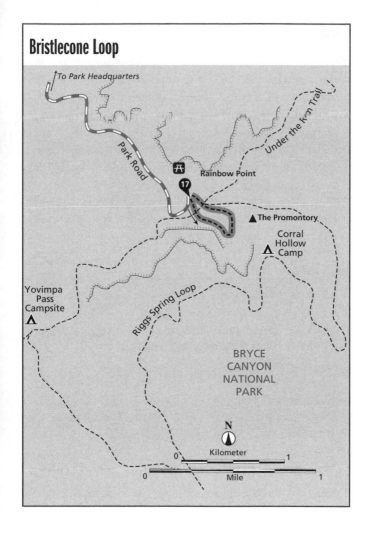

To Park Headquarters

Park Road

Under the Rim Trail

Rainbow Point

17

The Promontory

Corral Hollow Camp

Yovimpa Pass Campsite

Riggs Spring Loop

BRYCE CANYON NATIONAL PARK

N

Kilometer
0   1

Mile
0   1

The Hike

This short loop stays entirely above the canyon rim as it traverses a subalpine fir forest. The trail is named for the bristlecone pine, which is found more frequently along this trail than along other trails in Bryce Canyon National Park.

From the trailhead the path winds southeast through dense stands of white fir, Douglas fir, and ponderosa pine. The path loops out to the cliffs and the canyon rim. Bristlecone pines grow atop the open, windy cliffs along the rim. As the trail returns to Rainbow Point, it intersects the Under the Rim Trail. Trail signs along the route direct hikers back to the starting point.

Miles and Directions

0.0 Start at the Rainbow Point trailhead. Follow the path south.

0.1 Reach junction with Riggs Spring Loop.

0.8 Reach junction with the Under the Rim Trail. Follow trail signs for Rainbow Point to return to the trailhead.

1.0 Arrive back at the trailhead.

18 Mossy Cave

A short hike at the northeastern end of Bryce Canyon National Park.

Distance: 0.8 mile (1.2 km) round-trip
Approximate hiking time: 30 minutes
Best season: April through October
Difficulty: Easy
Water availability: Water Canyon typically holds water.
Hazards: Slippery stream crossings
Topo maps: Tropic Canyon (trail not shown); *Trails Illustrated*
Jurisdiction: Bryce Canyon National Park (See Appendix A for more information.)

Finding the trailhead: Drive Utah Highway 12 east from the junction with Utah Highway 63 to a marked pull-off on the south side of the road, 1.2 miles west of the park's east entrance.

The Hike

This trail offers a short stroll into the reddish pinnacles of Bryce Canyon from UT 12, offering a smaller-scale sampler of the grandeur to the south for travelers who do not wish to make the side trip into the main part of the park. The stream flows found here are not natural; pioneering settlers diverted water from the Sevier River into Water Canyon via a series of canals to feed croplands around Tropic.

The trail begins by following Water Canyon up into the breaks, with a wall of impressive pinnacles rising to the west. Soon the path reaches the first of two stream crossings. The crossings are usually easy rock-hops, but they can be tricky during spring runoff. Near the upper crossing,

Mossy Cave

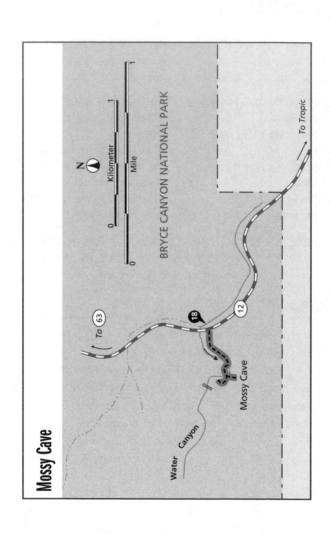

To 63

18

12

To Tropic

BRYCE CANYON NATIONAL PARK

N

Kilometer

Mile

0   1

0

Water Canyon

Mossy Cave

look up to view the natural arches and window walls in the cliffs to the west.

Once the second crossing is made, a short climb leads to a T intersection. To the right a short stroll leads to a 10-foot waterfall. To the left a brief but steep climb leads to Mossy Cave itself. This spacious alcove has been chiseled out by groundwater seeping through weaknesses in the bedrock. In winter the seeps feed impressive icicle gardens, while in summer the water provides sustenance for a vivid growth of mosses.

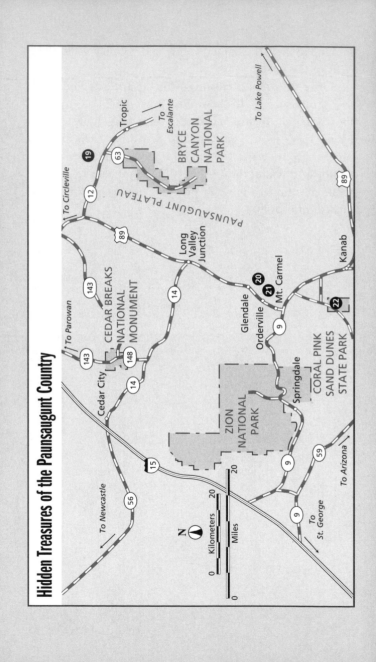

Hidden Treasures of the Paunsaugunt Country

Hidden Treasures of the Paunsaugunt Country

Bryce Canyon National Park occupies only a tiny corner of the vast Paunsaugunt Plateau, rimmed with rugged country that falls largely within the public domain. Countless hidden nooks and crannies here offer outstanding scenery, whether the view features the eroded red hoodoos of the uplands or the spectacular white cliffs of the Navajo Formation that gird the plateau's lower reaches. Most of these areas receive very low levels of visitation. It is here that travelers are most likely to avoid crowds and experience the wild solitude of a primeval landscape.

Most of the land falls under the direction of the Bureau of Land Management, which has local headquarters in Kanab. Several short day-hiking routes explore the western face of the Elkheart Cliffs.

19 Red Canyon Loop

A day-hiking route through Red Canyon encompassing portions of the Cassidy, Rich, and Ledge Point Trails in Dixie National Forest.

Distance: 4.0-mile (6.4 km) loop
Approximate hiking time: 2 hours
Best season: April through October
Difficulty: Moderate
Water availability: None

Hazards: Steep slopes, rocky surfaces
Topo maps: Wilson Peak, Casto Canyon
Jurisdiction: Powell Ranger District, Dixie National Forest (See Appendix A for more information.)

Finding the trailhead: From U.S. Highway 89 drive east on Utah Highway 12. Continue 1 mile east from the Red Canyon Visitor Center to a paved turnoff for the Cassidy trailhead on the north side of UT 12. A parking area, horse corral, information board, and pit toilet are located at the trailhead.

The Hike

This moderate route is pieced together with portions of the Cassidy, Rich, and Ledge Point Trails, making a loop through Red Canyon. These trails are also used by horse parties from April through October. Hikers who encounter horses on the trail should step aside and yield the right-of-way.

The route begins at the Cassidy trailhead at the northwest end of the parking lot. The path heads north, paralleling a wash through an arid landscape of ponderosa pine, limber pine, manzanita, and juniper. The terrain is rugged;

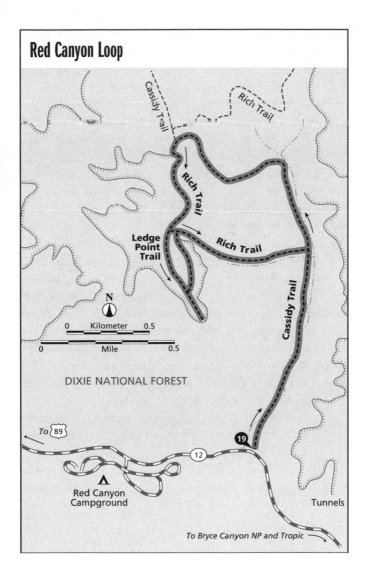

Red Canyon Loop

Cassidy Trail

Rich Trail

Rich Trail

Rich Trail

Ledge
Point
Trail

Cassidy Trail

N

Kilometer
0   0.5

Mile
0   0.5

DIXIE NATIONAL FOREST

To 89

19

Red Canyon
Campground

12

Tunnels

To Bryce Canyon NP and Tropic

pink limestone scree slopes border the wash. Like those of Bryce Canyon and the Cedar Breaks, the formations visible through Red Canyon are predominantly white and pink limestone from the Claron Formation. About 0.5 mile up the wash, the first pink limestone hoodoo formations come into view.

About 0.8 mile from the trailhead, hikers reach a first junction with the Rich Trail. Bear right, staying on the Cassidy Trail. The trail continues along the streamcourse to a confluence of several washes. Here the trail turns left and heads up a gradual-to-moderate slope to surmount a small hill. The path briefly follows the ridgeline. As you make upward progress, notice the resistant rock formations along the ridges to the left and right. Douglas firs grow in these higher elevations.

While still up in the high country, the Cassidy Trail reaches a second intersection with the Rich Trail. Break from the Cassidy Trail and follow the Rich Trail to the left (south). This portion of trail goes through a saddle, then descends along a draw that lies just west of the ridge that bears the Cassidy Trail. Along the descent the trail passes by The Gap, a wash between two resistant buttes.

Beyond The Gap, the trail ascends partway up another wash, then cuts across to another saddle, heading toward the Ledge Point Trail. The Ledge Point Trail is a horseshoe loop that intersects with the Rich Trail at two points. The loop brings hikers to Ledge Point, a picturesque overlook of the Red Canyon area with UT 12 visible below and to the south.

Follow the right (east) leg of the horseshoe loop back to the Rich Trail. Turn right and descend a slope that passes under cliffs of variegated sandstone above a watercourse.

This portion of the trail is quite rocky, with gravel and cobblestones. The trail briefly parallels the wash below, then descends rapidly to the streambed via a series of steep switchbacks. Along this portion of the trail are good examples of pink hoodoos and alcoves that border the wash. At the end of the draw, the path rejoins the Cassidy Trail. Backtrack southward along this portion of trail to return to the trailhead.

Miles and Directions

0.0 Start at the Cassidy trailhead.

0.8 At the junction with the Rich Trail, stay right on the Cassidy Trail.

1.7 At the second junction with the Rich Trail, turn left onto it.

2.1 Reach junction with the Ledge Point Trail. Turn right for a spur loop.

3.2 At junction with the Cassidy Trail, turn right.

4.0 Arrive back at the trailhead.

20 Red Hollow

An out-and-back wilderness route up a short, picturesque canyon.

Distance: 1.8 miles (2.9 km) round-trip

Approximate hiking time: 1 hour

Best season: April through October

Difficulty: Easy

Water availability: None

Hazards: Some scrambling over uneven surfaces, flash-flood danger

Topo maps: Orderville, Glendale

Jurisdiction: Bureau of Land Management, Kanab Field Office (See Appendix A for more information.)

Finding the trailhead: Follow U.S. Highway 89 to Orderville. Turn east on 100 East Street at the Centennial School. Turn left (north) on Red Hollow Drive. Drive 0.15 mile to a sand/gravel road. Follow the sand road 0.3 mile to a small turnout where a cement reservoir atop a small foothill should be in view. The hike begins by heading into the opening of a small canyon that is overlooked by pad-mounted transformers and a cement reservoir.

The Hike

This trail begins on the outskirts of Orderville and provides easy access to a deep canyon in the bone-white Elkheart Cliffs. As the route enters the mouth of the canyon, a high bank presents itself on the left side. It soon gives way to red cliffs that extend down to the canyon floor. The canyon soon splits into two short branches, each of which invites further exploration. Both branches are wooded with Gambel oak, juniper, and ponderosa pine. Hikers should not attempt to

Red Hollow

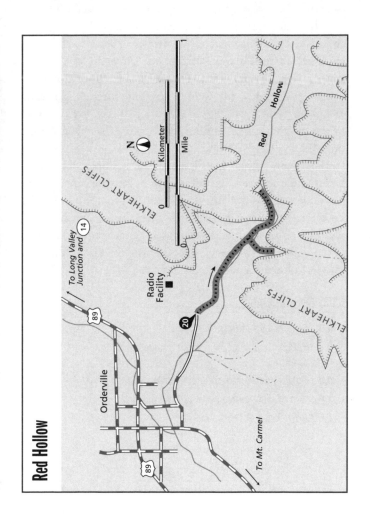

climb onto the sloping canyon walls; they may be easy to ascend, but they are almost impossible to get back down.

The south branch of the canyon breaks away to the right and has a somewhat narrow watercourse. Sheer cliffs of red sandstone form the walls of this side canyon. Cobblestones and sand line the narrow watercourse, making for easy traveling. At the end of this branch are some interesting natural arch formations overhanging the wash. At the very headwall of the canyon, a freestanding leaf of stone has been carved out of the cliffs by erosion.

The main branch is called Red Hollow. Heading up it, hikers will find crimson walls that slant into the canyon floor on the left, while overhanging walls with solution holes rise on the right. The walls of this branch narrow abruptly to a width of 6 feet or so and become impassable after a distance of 0.8 mile from the parking area. This is the end of the trek; travelers must now retrace their route.

Miles and Directions

0.0   Start at end of improved road.
0.7   Reach confluence with wash coming in from the right (south).
0.9   Reach headwall of the southern canyon.
1.0   End of main canyon and turnaround point.
1.8   Arrive back at the trailhead.

21 Sugar Knoll–Red Cave

A day hike to Sugar Knoll or Red Cave.

Distance: 4.2 miles (6.8 km) round-trip to Sugar Knoll; 3.6 miles (5.8 km) round trip to Red Cave
Approximate hiking time: 3 hours round-trip to Sugar Knoll
Best season: March through November
Difficulty: Moderate
Water availability: The potholes within Red Cave always contain murky water.
Hazards: Extreme flash flood danger within Red Cave
Topo map: Mount Carmel
Jurisdiction: Bureau of Land Management, Kanab Field Office (See Appendix A for more information.)

Finding the trailhead: From Orderville drive south on U.S. Highway 89 to the historic schoolhouse at Mile 83.5. Park here and hike north along the highway for 0.2 mile to a dirt road that runs eastward to the river. This road is the beginning of the hike.

The Hike

This route offers several manageable day-hiking options, visiting the spectacular high country at the base of the Elkheart Cliffs. These destinations are well known to local residents but receive little attention from others, so these hikes offer a fairly good opportunity for solitude. The Sugar Knoll route travels right to the base of the Elkheart Cliffs, while the Red Cave route visits an impossibly narrow slot canyon carved into red sandstone.

The hike initially follows a dirt road that runs eastward across the Long Valley. It soon makes an ankle-deep ford of the East Fork of the Virgin River. On the far bank the road swings north along the river for a time, then jogs east again

Sugar Knoll–Red Cave

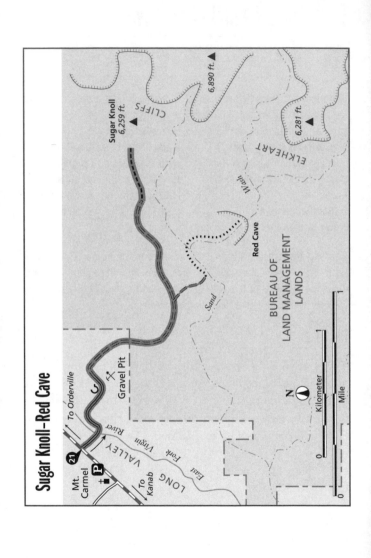

to reach a corral and gravel pit at the base of the hills. The route then follows a jeep track that rounds the corral on a northward heading and soon climbs to the top of a low plateau. Along the way are fine views of the Long Valley's fertile bottomlands.

Once the jeep road reaches the top of the plateau, a scrub forest of juniper allows only brief glimpses of the bone-white Elkheart Cliffs to the east. The jeep trail meanders through the scrub and breaks out onto a sagebrush flat just before reaching the Bureau of Land Management land boundary.

The track then makes its way to the edge of a steep bluff. Far below, a sandy wash issues from the red rock layers that underlie the Elkheart Cliffs. This arroyo is known as Sand Wash, and at its head is the slot canyon known locally as Red Cave. A second jeep trail soon drops away to the right to begin a journey up this canyon (see Red Cave Option, below).

Bear left at the fork for Sugar Knoll as the main jeep trail continues to climb gently toward the base of the cliffs. After 1.4 miles the jeep road ends and a rough trail bears east-northeast toward a red rock hoodoo. Follow this trail as it climbs across the slickrock to reach an overlook that offers a sweeping view of Sugar Knoll, with the Elkheart Cliffs providing a stunning backdrop. The junipers fall away as the trail drops onto sand dunes that have been stabilized by a growth of sagebrush, manzanita, and Gambel oak.

Expect sandy hiking conditions as the trail covers the remaining distance to the base of Sugar Knoll. Here, beneath a small blowout cave in the bedrock, the path splits into a tangle of sandy avenues that entice further exploration along the base of this striking butte of wind-sculpted sandstone.

Miles and Directions

0.0 Start where the dirt road departs US 89.

0.2 Road fords the East Fork of the Virgin River.

0.4 Pass a gravel pit. Follow jeep trail to the north.

1.1 Jeep trail enters BLM lands.

1.2 Jeep trail splits. Turn right for Red Cave (1.2 miles out and back, moderate); bear left for Sugar Knoll.

1.8 Jeep trail ends. Follow rough path to the northeast.

2.1 Reach base of Sugar Knoll.

4.2 Return to trailhead.

Red Cave Option: From the blufftop junction of jeep trails, follow the track that descends steeply into the valley of Sand Wash. As its name implies, the wash is a wide avenue of sand that has been deposited by eons of flash flooding. Traveling is easy as the route follows the wash upward toward its source, an impossibly narrow declivity in the red lower layers of Navajo sandstone. This is the slot canyon called Red Cave, and hikers can penetrate it for only a short distance without vigorous climbing. Out and back to the Red Cave adds 1.2 miles (about 45 minutes) to the Sugar Knoll hike. The hike from the trailhead to Red Cave only is 3.6 miles (about 3 hours).

Deep pools of water form in the floor of the cleft and are always cold—wear a wetsuit for extended exploration. Whorled walls rise up to block the sky, and the canyon floor is only wide enough to admit travelers in single file. This narrow chasm is a death trap when waters reach flood stage, since hikers have no way to climb upward. Visitors should carefully monitor the weather conditions and enter the slot canyon only if cloudless skies are a certainty.

22 Coral Pink Sand Dunes

A day-hiking loop onto the ridges overlooking the dynamic Coral Pink Sand Dunes, returning through the dune fields themselves.

Distance: 2.5-mile (4.0 km) loop
Approximate hiking time: 2 hours
Best season: April through November
Difficulty: Moderately strenuous
Water availability: None

Hazards: Steep slopes with uneven footing
Topo map: Yellow Jacket Canyon
Jurisdiction: Bureau of Land Management, Kanab Field Office; Coral Pink Sand Dunes State Park (See Appendix A for more information.)

Finding the trailhead: From Mount Carmel Junction drive south on U.S. Highway 89 to a sign marked CORAL PINK SAND DUNES. Turn right on County Road 1850 and drive 9.3 miles to a large, open area used for four-wheel-drive recreation on the left (east) side of the road.

The Hike

Note: The dunes are used frequently by off-road vehicles. Hikers are welcome but should exercise caution.

The Coral Pink Sand Dunes offer an infinite array of possible route choices. The dunes occupy a long, narrow valley overlooked by sandstone hills to the east. As a result of prevailing winds, the dunes are oriented along an east-west axis. Travel is easiest along the axis of the dunes; hikers on a north-south heading will face numerous up and downs. A few loosely defined jeep tracks trace the edges of the dunes, but the heart of this miniature Sahara is essentially trailless.

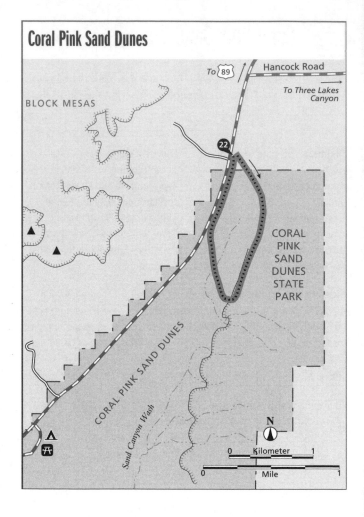

Coral Pink Sand Dunes

BLOCK MESAS

To 89

Hancock Road

To Three Lakes Canyon

22

CORAL PINK SAND DUNES STATE PARK

CORAL PINK SAND DUNES

Sand Canyon Wash

N

0 Kilometer 1

0 Mile 1

Our route climbs onto the ridges west of the dunes for an aerial view before descending into the heart of the dunes for the return trip.

From the parking area, head southeast over the sand dunes toward the sandstone hills bordering the valley. These hills are wooded in an open scrub of ponderosa pine and juniper. Wherever possible, stay on the four-wheel-drive tracks as you walk for easiest traveling. This will spare the delicate vegetation growing on the unstable slopes of the dunes. Watch the undisturbed surface of the sand for animal tracks and patterns made by the wind.

As you gain elevation and approach the sandstone foothills, notice that the dunes are partially stabilized by populations of ponderosa pine, sagebrush, yucca, and a variety of small desert plants. As the route climbs into the hills, limber pine, Gambel oak, and manzanita populations become prevalent.

Once up on the sandstone, head south along the foothills toward a gorge that penetrates the rock. This portion of the trek provides an excellent vantage point from which to look out over the dunes and study their patterns. Just before the gorge, a few shallow washes head southward. Explore these, but proceed with caution—the washes end abruptly with a rapid descent into the gorge.

Descend into the dunes, choosing a route slightly north of the gorge. Investigate your route before beginning a descent in order to avoid thickets of Gambel oak and manzanita. Spending a few minutes studying the east-west pattern of the dunes will help you end your descent within a trough or on the crest of a dune. The trough or crest can then be followed back toward the parking area.

Sagebrush flats and a barbed-wire fence guard the western border of the state park. Angle northwest to encounter this fence, and follow it north through the sagebrush to return to the parking area.

Miles and Directions

0.0 Start at parking area.

1.3 Reach a deep gorge through the sandstone hills. Turn west and descend into the sand dunes.

2.5 The route returns to the parking area.

Appendix A: Managing Agencies

Bureau of Land Management
Kanab Field Office
318 North 100 East
Kanab, UT 84741
(435) 544–2672
www.ut.blm.gov/kanab_fo

St. George Field Office
345 East Riverside Drive
St. George, UT 84790
(435) 688–3200
www.ut.blm.gov/st_george

USDA Forest Service
Powell Ranger District
225 East Center
P.O. Box 80
Panguitch, UT 84759
(435) 676–8815

Supervisor
Dixie National Forest
82 North 100 East
Cedar City, UT 84720
(435) 865–3700
www.fs.fed.us/dxnf

National Park Service
Bryce Canyon National Park
Bryce Canyon, UT 84717
(435) 834–5322
www.nps.gov/brca

Cedar Breaks National Monument
P.O. Box 749
Cedar City, UT 84720
(435) 586–9451
www.nps.gov/cebr

Zion National Park
Springdale, UT 84767-1099
(435) 772–3256
www.nps.gov/zion

State of Utah
Coral Pink Sand Dunes State Park
P.O. Box 95
Kanab, UT 84741
(435) 648–2800
www.utah.com/stateparks/coral_pink.htm

Appendix B: Day Hiker Checklist

Use this list to create your own, based on the nature of your hike and personal needs.

Clothing
- [ ] dependable rain parka
- [ ] wind-resistant jacket
- [ ] wetsuit (for canyon wading in cold weather)
- [ ] thermal underwear
- [ ] shorts
- [ ] long pants
- [ ] cap or hat
- [ ] wool shirt or sweater
- [ ] warm jacket
- [ ] extra socks
- [ ] underwear
- [ ] lightweight shirts
- [ ] T-shirts
- [ ] wool gloves

Footwear
- [ ] comfortable hiking boots
- [ ] lightweight camp shoes
- [ ] water shoes or sandals

Food & Drink
- [ ] trail mix
- [ ] snacks
- [ ] water

Photography

- [ ] camera
- [ ] film
- [ ] accessories
- [ ] dry bag

Miscellaneous

- [ ] maps, compasses
- [ ] wading staff
- [ ] toilet paper
- [ ] small trowel or shovel
- [ ] water filter or purifier
- [ ] first-aid kit
- [ ] survival kit
- [ ] pocket knife
- [ ] insect repellent
- [ ] flashlight, with spare batteries and bulb
- [ ] extra plastic bags to pack out trash
- [ ] waterproof covering for pack
- [ ] binoculars
- [ ] watch
- [ ] this hiking guide

About the Authors

Erik Molvar discovered backpacking while working on a volunteer trail crew in the North Cascades of Washington. His experiences led him to choose a career in the outdoors, and he soon found himself studying wildlife biology at the University of Montana. His studies there were followed by a master of science degree from the University of Alaska, Fairbanks, where his groundbreaking research on the behavior and ecology of moose was published in several international journals. Erik is currently the director of Biodiversity Conservation Alliance, a nonprofit conservation group in Wyoming. His other FalconGuides include *Hiking Arizona's Cactus Country, Hiking the Bob Marshall Country, Hiking Colorado's Maroon Bells–Snowmass Wilderness, Hiking Glacier and Waterton Lakes National Park, Hiking the North Cascades, Hiking Olympic National Park, Hiking Wyoming's Cloud Peak Wilderness, Hiking Zion & Bryce Canyon National Parks,* and *Wild Wyoming.* He also is the author of *Scenic Driving Alaska and the Yukon* (The Globe Pequot Press) and *Alaska on Foot: Wilderness Techniques for the Far North* (Countryman Press).

Tamara Martin holds a bachelor of science in environmental health from Westchester University in Pennsylvania. After graduation she began her professional career as an environmental consultant in southeast Texas. In pursuit of her dreams, she took a sabbatical to spend a summer hiking in Denali National Park. She currently works as a ranger for Moran State Park and as a part-time sea-kayaking guide in the San Juan Islands of Washington.